Red Line **6**

Vokabellernheft

Ausgabe für Bayern

Herausgeber: Dr. Frank Haß

Ernst Klett Verlag
Stuttgart • Leipzig • Dortmund

Vorwort

Liebe Schülerin, lieber Schüler,

mit diesem Vokabellernheft im praktischen Taschenformat kannst du überall deine Wörter lernen, wiederholen und nachschlagen.

In den Wortlisten kannst du Wörter und Wendungen, die dir schwierig vorkommen, mit Textmarker oder Bleistift markieren, um sie dann immer wieder durchzugehen.

Auch die vielen Übungen nach jedem Lektionsteil unterstützen dich bei der Wiederholung. So kannst du dich prima auf Tests und Prüfungen vorbereiten.

Hinter jedem Wort ist die Lautschrift (z. B. [ˈplænɪt] für planet) angegeben. Diese hilft dir, wenn du nicht weißt, wie du das Wort aussprechen sollst.

Hilfreiche Hinweise zum Umgang mit den Lautschriftzeichen findest du in deinem Englischbuch ab Seite 222 am unteren Rand aller *Dictionary*-Seiten.

Viel Erfolg beim Vokabellernen!

Zoom in A world language

p. 8	**primary** ['praɪmri]	*hier:* Erst-; primär
	auxiliary [ɔ:g'zɪljri]	Hilfs-
	native speaker [ˌneɪtɪv 'spi:kə]	Muttersprachler; Muttersprachlerin
	even if ['i:vn̩ˌɪf]	auch wenn
	for instance [fərˌ'ɪnstəns]	zum Beispiel
	e-waste ['i:weɪst]	Elektronikschrott
	relatively ['relətɪvli]	relativ; vergleichsweise
	in comparison to [ɪn kəm'pærɪsn̩ tə]	im Vergleich zu
	least [li:st]	geringste; am wenigsten
	flight attendant ['flaɪtˌəˌtendnt]	Flugbegleiter; Flugbegleiterin
	the Philippines [ðə 'fɪlɪpi:nz]	die Philippinen
	Nigeria [naɪ'dʒɪəriə]	Nigeria
	to store [stɔ:]	speichern; aufbewahren; lagern
	worldwide [ˌwɜ:ld'waɪd]	weltweit
	sailor ['seɪlə]	Seemann; Matrose
	to control [kən'trəʊl]	kontrollieren; steuern
	significant [sɪg'nɪfɪkənt]	bedeutend; wesentlich
	economically [ˌi:kə'nɒmɪkli]	wirtschaftlich; sparsam
	growth [grəʊθ]	Wachstum
p. 9	**spoon** [spu:n]	Löffel
	fork [fɔ:k]	Gabel
	alcoholic [ˌælkə'hɒlɪk]	alkoholisch; Alkohol-
	handbag ['hænbæg]	Handtasche
	working from home [ˌwɜ:kɪŋ frəm 'həʊm]	im Homeoffice arbeiten; von zu Hause aus arbeiten
	audition [ɔ:'dɪʃn]	Vorspielen; Vorsprechen; Vorsingen; Vortanzen
	cell phone *(AE)* ['sel ˌfəʊn]	Mobiltelefon; Handy

1 Find the words.

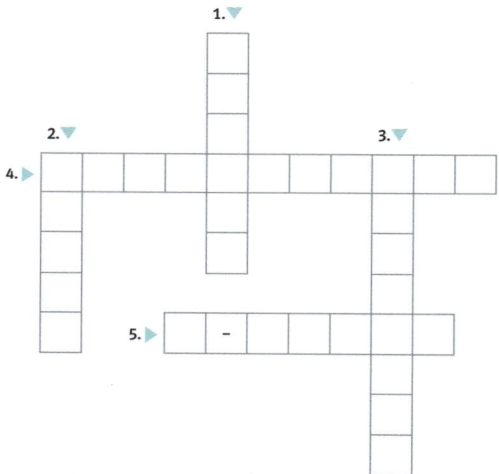

▼ 1. The language you learn as a child, usually from your parents, is your ... language.

2. You eat soup with a ….

3. Actors and singers often have to do an ... to get a job.

▶ 4. Another word for important is ….

5. Old phones, laptops and other technology are called ….

2 Write the words in English.

1. _____

2. _____

3. _____

4.  _____

3 Put the words into the right sentences.

auxiliary   Even if   audition   store

instance   relatively

1. I know lots of people who have lived abroad.

   For _____ , my brother lived in Spain for

   a year.

2. I have an _____ for a new play at the

   weekend.

3. _____ it rains, I still want to go to the

   beach.

4. Where can we _____ our bags?

5. This hotel is _____ cheap.

6. English is often used as an _____

   language.

Unit 1 The rainbow nation

| p. 10 | **nation** ['neɪʃn] | Nation; Land; Staat |

Intro

p. 10	**diverse** [daɪ'vɜːs]	vielfältig; breitgefächert
	safari [sə'fɑːri]	Safari
	buffalo *(sg)*, **buffaloes** *(pl)*	Büffel
	leopard ['lepəd]	Leopard; Leopardin
	lion ['laɪən]	Löwe
	rhino ['raɪnəʊ]	Rhinozeros; Nashorn
	natural ['nætʃrl]	Natur-; natürlich
p. 11	**World Cup** [ˌwɜːld 'kʌp]	Weltmeisterschaft
	final ['faɪnl]	Finale
	to **unite** [ju:'naɪt]	vereinen; vereinigen
	South African	Südafrikaner; Südafrikanerin;
	[ˌsaʊθˌ'æfrɪkən]	südafrikanisch; aus Südafrika
	the Dutch [ðə 'dʌtʃ]	die Niederländer
	apartheid *(no pl)* [ə'pɑːtaɪt]	Apartheid
	to **separate** ['sepreɪt]	trennen
	exclusive [ɪks'kluːsɪv]	exklusiv
	gated community	bewachte Wohnanlage;
	[ˌgeɪtɪd kə'mjuːnəti]	geschlossene Wohnanlage
	township ['taʊnʃɪp]	Township *(Siedlung in Süd-afrika, in der vor allem sozial schlechtergestellte Menschen leben)*
p. 10	**living conditions**	Lebensbedingungen
	['lɪvɪŋ kənˌdɪʃnz]	
p. 11	to **migrate** [maɪ'greɪt]	abwandern; umsiedeln

Keep moving!
After practising new words,
go for a walk and try to
remember as many of them
as possible.

1 Write the words in English.

1. _____

2. _____

3. _____

4. _____

2 Complete the interview.

Interviewer: Excuse me, can I ask you a question?

Do you remember when South Africa won the

1995 W__ __ __ __ C __ __?

Zama: Of course I do! It was the first time I felt like South

Africa could really be one n__ __ __ __ __. I think sporting

events can really u__ __ __ __ people.

Interviewer: I agree. It was an important day for

all S__ __ __ __ A__ __ __ __ __ __ __. It gave people

hope that life would get better after so many years of

a__ __ __ __ __ __ __ __, don't you think?

Zama: Yes, although we have to remember that the country

isn't perfect yet. Some people still have terrible

l__ __ __ __ __ c__ __ __ __ __ __ __ __, while others live

in e__ __ __ __ __ __ __ __ areas.

Interviewer: That's true. It's great that South Africa is such

a d__ __ __ __ __ __ country, but we still have some problems

that need to be solved.

3 Match the sentence parts.

1. The Dutch	a) when we were on safari.
2. During apartheid	b) many people migrated to South Africa from the North.
3. We saw lots of animals	c) live in townships like Soweto.
4. Many South Africans	d) arrived in South Africa in the 17th century.
5. Around 1,000 years ago	e) different groups of the population were separated.

4 Complete the advert.

safarifeuniteanationgrpaznaturalfsyseparatediuliunitec

INTERNET

Experience South Africa

Come to Kruger National Park and see animals in

their _____ environment! If you're lucky, you

might even see baby _____ at this time of year.

Book your _____ now!

If you're interested in the history of this

fascinating _____, visit the Apartheid Museum

in Johannesburg to learn about how the population

was _____ and how Nelson Mandela

tried to _____ the country after 1994.

Topic 1

p. 12	**coastline** [ˈkəʊstlaɪn]	Küste
	backdrop [ˈbækdrɒp]	Hintergrund
	scenery [ˈsiːnri]	Landschaft
	survey [ˈsɜːveɪ]	Umfrage
	to **strike** [straɪk]	*hier:* auffallen; treffen; ausbrechen
	Cape Dutch [ˌkeɪp ˈdʌtʃ]	kapholländisch
	cuisine [kwɪzˈiːn]	Küche
	available [əˈveɪləbl]	erhältlich; verfügbar
	spiced [spaɪst]	gewürzt; scharf
	minced meat [ˌmɪnst ˈmiːt]	Hackfleisch
	since [sɪns]	*hier:* da; weil
	plenty of [ˈplenti əv]	eine Menge
	seal [siːl]	Seehund; Robbe
	penguin [ˈpeŋgwɪn]	Pinguin
	glimpse [glɪms]	(kurzer/flüchtiger) Blick
	resident [ˈrezɪdnt]	Bewohner; Bewohnerin; Anwohner; Anwohnerin; Einwohner; Einwohnerin
	wealthy [ˈwelθi]	wohlhabend; reich
	to **get by** [ˌget ˈbaɪ]	auskommen
	ZAR *(= South African rand)* [rænd]	Rand *(südafrikanische Währungseinheit)*
	to **rise** [raɪz]	(auf)steigen; aufgehen
	unemployment *(no pl)* [ˌʌnɪmˈplɔɪmənt]	Arbeitslosigkeit
	rate [reɪt]	Rate; Quote
	to **patrol** [pəˈtrəʊl]	patrouillieren; Streife gehen
	complete [kəmˈpliːt]	vollständig
	perspective [pəˈspektɪv]	Perspektive; Blickwinkel
	handmade [ˌhænˈmeɪd]	handgefertigt
	souvenir [ˌsuːvnˈɪə]	Souvenir; Andenken
	to **make the most of sth** [ˌmeɪk ðə ˈməʊst əv]	etw. ausnutzen; das Beste aus etw. machen
	What's on? [ˌwɒts ˈɒn]	Was ist los?

	taste [teɪst]	Geschmack
	open-air [ˌəʊpn̩ˈeə]	Open-Air-; Freilicht-
	carnival [ˈkɑːnɪvl]	Karneval; Fasching
	among [əˈmʌŋ]	unter; inmitten
	household [ˈhaʊshəʊld]	Haushalt(s-)
	shack [ʃæk]	Baracke; Bretterbude
	running water [ˌrʌnɪŋ ˈwɔːtə]	fließendes Wasser
	flush [flʌʃ]	Spülung; Spül-
p. 13	**relaxed** [rɪˈlækst]	entspannt; locker; gelassen
	income [ˈɪnkʌm]	Einkommen(s-)
	access *(no pl)* [ˈækses]	Zugang; Zutritt
	electric [ɪˈlektrɪk]	elektrisch
	landline [ˈlændlaɪn]	Festnetz(telefon)
p. 14	to **reduce** [rɪˈdjuːs]	reduzieren; vermindern; verringern
	drug [drʌg]	Droge; Medikament
	the public [ðə ˈpʌblɪk]	die Öffentlichkeit
	crew [kruː]	Crew; Besatzung; Mannschaft
	dolphin [ˈdɒlfɪn]	Delfin
	to **show sb around (a place)** [ˌʃəʊ əˈraʊnd]	jmdn. (an einem Ort) herumführen
p. 15	**security** [sɪˈkjʊərəti]	Sicherheit

5 Write the words in English.

1. _____

2. _____

3. _____

4. _____

6 Complete the sentences with the right forms of the verbs.

get by   strike   rise   reduce

make the most of   show sb around

1. The thing that _____ me most about the city was how friendly the people were.

2. Lots of people have to _____ on very low wages.

3. In many towns, the population _____ at the moment.

4. We really _____ our time in South Africa – we saw something new every day!

5. Factories should try to _____ the amount of waste they produce.

6. Tomorrow morning, I will be _____ the city by a friend.

7 Match the words with their definitions.

1. resident   a) a list of questions which people answer

2. cuisine   b) because

3. open-air   c) someone who lives somewhere

4. backdrop   d) food

5. survey   e) outside

6. since   f) background

8 Complete the sentences and find the answer to 9.

1. The beautiful b __ __☐__ __ __ __ of Table Mountain is one of the things that makes Cape Town unique.

2. You can sometimes see whales and penguins on the

   c __☐__ __ __ __ __ __.

3. The police p __ __☐__ __ some areas of the city.

4. There are p __ __☐__ __ o __ Cape Dutch buildings to see.

5. You should try some of the traditional South African c__ __ __☐__ __.

6. It's a good idea to talk to local people to find out about their p __ __ __ __ __ __ __ ☐__ on life in Cape Town.

7. Many w __☐__ __ __ __ people live in exclusive gated communities.

8. U __ __ __ __☐__ __ __ __ __ is a problem in some parts of the city.

9. Every year there is a __ __ __ __ __ __ __ __ in Cape Town.

9 Find the words and complete the text.

a) Find six words.

R	E	S	I	D	E	N	T	S
E	L	N	U	I	E	M	D	G
L	A	N	D	L	I	N	E	A
A	E	G	W	N	L	E	D	C
X	H	I	N	C	O	M	E	C
E	L	U	C	G	L	A	J	E
D	A	I	F	L	U	S	H	S
S	R	T	R	V	O	E	L	S

b) Use the words to complete the text.

Many people in Cape Town have a r_____ lifestyle,

but for others, life can be hard. In some areas, lots

of houses do not have internet a_____,

a l_____ or a toilet with

a f_____.

The r_____ of these areas often have a very

low i_____ and have to work very hard just to

get by.

10 Find the wrong word.

1. running water • landline • minced meat • flush

2. coastline • survey • scenery • backdrop

3. souvenir • cuisine • carnival • unemployment

4. resident • seal • dolphin • penguin

Topic 2

p. 19	to **be in the making** [bɪˌɪn ðə ˈmeɪkɪŋ]	im Entstehen sein
	remarkable [rɪˈmɑːkəbl]	bemerkenswert; erstaunlich
	former [ˈfɔːmə]	ehemalige; frühere
	to **shake hands** [ˌʃeɪk ˈhændz]	Hände schütteln; sich die Hand geben
	Afrikaner [ˌæfrɪˈkɑːnə]	Afrikaander/-in *(weiße Menschen in Südafrika mit Afrikaans als Muttersprache)*
	captain [ˈkæptɪn]	Kapitän; Kapitänin
	to **despise** [dɪˈspaɪz]	verachten
	furthermore [ˌfɜːðəˈmɔː]	überdies; außerdem
	whichever [wɪˈtʃevə]	wer auch immer; was auch immer
	to **cheer** [tʃɪə]	jubeln; zujubeln; anfeuern
	slogan [ˈsləʊgən]	Slogan; Werbespruch
	to **lie ahead** [ˌlaɪ əˈhed]	noch kommen
	background [ˈbækgraʊnd]	Hintergrund
	political [pəˈlɪtɪkl]	politisch
	to **last** [lɑːst]	(an)dauern; anhalten
	Coloured [ˈkʌləd]	„Farbige/-r" *(inzwischen als diskriminierend empfundene Bezeichnung)*
	landless [ˈlændləs]	landlos
	economic [ˌiːkəˈnɒmɪk]	ökonomisch; wirtschaftlich
	neighbourhood [ˈneɪbəhʊd]	Nachbarschaft; Umgebung
	homeland [ˈhəʊmlænd]	Homeland *(Siedlungsgebiet für schwarze Menschen in Südafrika während der Apartheid)*
p. 20	**handshake** [ˈhænʃeɪk]	Händeschütteln; Händedruck
	to **marginalise** [ˈmɑːdʒɪnəlaɪz]	an den Rand drängen
	Personally, ... [ˈpɜːsnli]	Ich persönlich ...
	what's more [ˌwɒts ˈmɔː]	darüber hinaus
	politician [ˌpɒlɪˈtɪʃn]	Politiker; Politikerin
	constitution [kɒnstɪˈtjuːʃn]	Verfassung

cooperation [kəʊˌɒpəˈreɪʃn]		Kooperation; Zusammenarbeit
inequality [ˌɪnɪˈkwɒləti]		Ungleichheit
p. 21 **democratic** [ˌdeməˈkrætɪk]		demokratisch
reaction [riˈækʃn]		Reaktion
celebration [ˌseləˈbreɪʃn]		Feier
jersey [ˈdʒɜːzi]		Trikot
calm [kɑːm]		ruhig; friedlich
by the time [baɪ ðə ˈtaɪm]		bis; als
to **fill up** [ˌfɪlˈʌp]		(auf)füllen; sich füllen
to **go wild** [ˌgəʊ ˈwaɪld]		außer sich geraten
fireworks *(pl)* [ˈfaɪəwɜːks]		Feuerwerk

11 Put the words into the table.

calm · cheer · marginalise · former · inequality

despise · economic · neighbourhood · constitution

last · background · remarkable

Nouns	Verbs	Adjectives

12 **Complete the news report.**

> *Evening News*   *24-06-1995*
>
> # Hope for the new nation
>
> Today was a r_____ day for all South
>
> Africans, and shows that a better future
>
> l_____ a_____ .
>
> When Nelson Mandela s_____ h_____
>
> with the c_____ of the rugby team, Francois
>
> Pienaar, he showed that he wanted South Africa to become
>
> a d_____
>
> country with c_____ between all
>
> groups of society. W_____ m_____ , the
>
> r_____ when South Africa won the match shows
>
> that people feel proud of their country. After the match,
>
> there were c_____ and
>
> f_____ .

13 **Write the words in English.**

1.  _____

2.  _____

3. _____

4. _____

14 Complete the text.

The young politics blog

I believe that everyone has the right to

live in a de _____ society. It's

important that we all have the same rights

and ec _____ opportunities.

Furthermore, we need honest po _____

who really care about us, and there should also be

better co _____ between political

parties.

Olivia, 16

Pe _____ , I think that there are lots of

problems with our political system.

In the co _____ , it says that everyone

is equal, but there is still in _____ in many

areas of life. Lots of people are ma _____

and have to work much harder than

others to achieve what they want.

Curtis, 18

15 Complete the sentences with the right forms of the verbs.

lie ahead   fill up   marginalise   shake hands   go wild

1. Society should not _____ any

   individuals or groups.

2. When the South African football team scored, the

   crowd _____ .

3. Difficult times _____ , but we shouldn't

   give up.

4. The two captains _____ before the match.

5. The stadium always _____ very quickly

   before a match.

16 Match the words with their definitions.

1. the opposite of angry or excited   a) cooperation

2. when people work together   b) captain

3. an area where people live   c) landless

4. a leader, for example of a sports team   d) despise

5. to hate   e) calm

6. without land   f) neighbourhood

Text 2

p. 23	**opposite** ['ɒpəzɪt]	Gegenteil
	to **announce** [ə'naʊns]	ankündigen; verkünden
	Xhosa ['kɔːsə]	Xhosa *(Sprache)*
	stick fighting ['stɪk ˌfaɪtɪŋ]	Stockkampf
	boxing ['bɒksɪŋ]	Boxen
	impact ['ɪmpækt]	Einfluss; Auswirkung
	wife *(sg)*, **wives** *(pl)*	Ehefrau
	besides [bɪ'saɪdz]	außerdem; außer
	to **pronounce** [prə'naʊns]	aussprechen
	control [kən'trəʊl]	Kontrolle; Steuerung
	university [ˌjuːnɪ'vɜːsəti]	Universität
	fair [feə]	gerecht; fair
p. 24	**massacre** ['mæsəkə]	Massaker
	party ['pɑːti]	*hier:* Partei; Gruppe
	to **torture** ['tɔːtʃə]	foltern; quälen
	involved [ɪn'vɒlvd]	engagiert; beteiligt
	to **injure** ['ɪndʒə]	verletzen
	military ['mɪlɪtri]	militärisch; Militär-
	sabotage ['sæbətɑːʒ]	Sabotage
	for life [fə 'laɪf]	lebenslänglich
	divorce [dɪ'vɔːs]	Scheidung
	funeral ['fjuːnrəl]	Beerdigung; Begräbnis
p. 25	**bombing** ['bɒmɪŋ]	Bombardierung; Bombenanschlag
	well-known [ˌwel'nəʊn]	wohl bekannt
	pressure ['preʃə]	Druck
	to **release** [rɪ'liːs]	*hier:* entlassen; freisetzen; loslassen; veröffentlichen
	to **heal** [hiːl]	heilen
	to **divorce sb** [dɪ'vɔːs]	sich von jmdm. scheiden lassen
	to **retire** [rɪ'taɪə]	sich zurückziehen; sich zur Ruhe setzen
	public ['pʌblɪk]	öffentlich

publicity [pʌb'lɪsəti]	Publicity; Reklame; Aufmerksamkeit
to **appear** [ə'pɪə]	auftauchen; erscheinen
TB (= tuberculosis) [ˌtiː'biː, tʃuːˌbɜːkjə'ləʊsɪs]	Tbc (= Tuberkulose)
to **regard** [rɪ'gɑːd]	betrachten
extraordinary [ɪk'strɔːdnri]	außergewöhnlich
to **name** [neɪm]	nennen; benennen
to **raise** [reɪz]	*hier:* einwerben
to **overcome** [ˌəʊvə'kʌm]	überwinden
justice ['dʒʌstɪs]	Gerechtigkeit; Justiz
grandson ['grænsʌn]	Enkel(sohn)
duty ['djuːti]	Pflicht
p. 26 to **campaign (for)** [kæm'peɪn (fə)]	demonstrieren (für); sich engagieren (für); aufmerksam machen (auf)
unexpected [ˌʌnɪk'spektɪd]	unerwartet
sibling ['sɪblɪŋ]	Geschwister
to **welcome** ['welkəm]	begrüßen; willkommen heißen
to **remind sb of/about sth/sb** [rɪ'maɪnd]	(jmdn. an etw./jmdn.) erinnern
determination *(no pl)* [dɪˌtɜːmɪ'neɪʃn]	Entschlossenheit

17 Put the words into the table.

heal   fair   determination   unexpected

pronounce   wife   duty   retire   extraordinary

Nouns	Verbs	Adjectives

18 Complete the text.

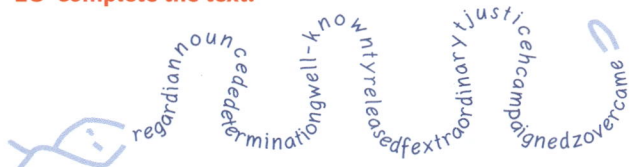

regardiannouncedetermniationgwell-knowntyreleasedfextraordinarytjusticehcampaignedzovercame

When Nelson Mandela's death was _____ ,

people in South Africa and all over the world wanted to

remember and celebrate the life of this _____

man. Many _____ him as a hero because

he worked to end apartheid and _____

huge challenges. Although he was in prison for almost 27 years,

he never lost his _____ to make his

country fairer for everyone.

After he was _____ from prison, he

became president of South Africa and countinued to fight

for _____ .

He also _____

for better support for people with

AIDS. Today, he is

_____

as a politician and is a role model

for many people.

19 Complete the radio interview.

Interviewer: Today, I would like to w_____ Professor

Nkosi to the studio. Professor Nkosi, you're an expert

on the history of apartheid and Nelson Mandela's life.

What i_____ did Mandela's time in prison have on his

family life?

Professor Nkosi: Well, in 1958, Mandela had

d_____ his first wife and married Winifred

Madikizela. It was very difficult for him to not see Winnie for

so long. Then one of his sons was killed and he couldn't even

go to the f_____. I think Mandela's strength in this

situation is e_____.

Interviewer: Yes, we can't even imagine how difficult that

was. Now, we all know that Nelson Mandela became president

after he was r_____ from prison. There was

lots of pu_____ at the time and he became a hero for

a lot of people. But what happened after that?

Professor Nkosi: Mandela didn't r_____ from

p_____ life after his political career. Instead, he

continued to work for peace and also fought against AIDS.

His charity, which was n_____ after his old prison

number, r_____ money through international concerts.

I think his life should help to r_____ us of what we

can do to help others and to c_____ for a better

society.

Unit 2 Living in a global village

Intro

p. 34	**planet** ['plænɪt]	Planet
	half *(sg)*, **halves** *(pl)*	(die) Hälfte
	to **identify** [aɪ'dentɪfaɪ]	(sich) identifizieren
	senior ['si:nɪə]	Senior; Seniorin
	refugee [ˌrefjʊ'dʒi:]	Flüchtling
	drinking water ['drɪŋkɪŋ ˌwɔ:tə]	Trinkwasser
	CO₂ emissions *(pl)* [ˌsi:əʊ'tu:ˌiˌmɪʃnz]	CO₂-Ausstoß
p. 35	**Mandarin** ['mændrɪn]	Mandarin *(Sprache)*
	Arabic ['ærəbɪk]	arabisch; Arabisch
	to **remain** [rɪ'meɪn]	übrig bleiben; bleiben
	a third [ə 'θɜ:d]	ein Drittel
	literacy *(no pl)* ['lɪtrəsi]	Lese- und Schreibfähigkeit
	illiterate [ɪ'lɪtrət]	Analphabet; Analphabetin; analphabetisch *(des Lesens und Schreibens unkundig)*
	employment [ɪm'plɔɪmənt]	Beschäftigung; Anstellung
	sector ['sektə]	Sektor; Bereich; Zone
	nevertheless [ˌnevəðə'les]	trotzdem; dennoch; nichtsdestoweniger
	due to ['dju: tə]	infolge von; wegen
	flood [flʌd]	Flut; Hochwasser; Überschwemmung
	drought [draʊt]	Dürre; Trockenheit
	crop [krɒp]	Feldfrucht; Ernte
	overweight [ˌəʊvə'weɪt]	übergewichtig
	malnourished [ˌmæl'nʌrɪʃt]	unterernährt
	obese [ə'bi:s]	fett(leibig)
p. 34	**native language** [ˌneɪtɪv 'læŋgwɪdʒ]	Muttersprache

1 Write the words in English.

1. 茶道   M _____

2. مدرسة   A _____

3.   P _____

4.   s _____

2 Complete the text.

There are around 8 billion people on our p_____ and

they all have very different lives. Around 1 % of people

are r_____ who have had to leave their

homes d_____ t_____ war or violence, or because of

extreme weather like f_____ or d_____.

On the other hand, some people have a life with lots

of luxuries, and around 39 % of the world's population

is o_____ or even o_____. Another

area where there is also inequality is l_____. In some

countries, almost everyone can read and write, while in others,

many people are i_____.

3 Put the words into the table.

half   planet   illiterate   identify   disappear

overweight   a third   healthy   remain

Nouns	Verbs	Adjectives
_____	_____	_____
_____	_____	_____
_____	_____	_____

4 Complete the sentences.

1. Water which is safe to drink is ....   a) due to

2. The language with the most native   b) malnourished
   speakers in the world is ...

3. Being able to read and write is ....   c) employment

4. When you have a job, you have ....   d) sector

5. An area or type of work is a ....   e) literacy

6. Another word for 'because of' is ....   f) drinking water

7. When someone doesn't have   g) Mandarin
   enough food, they are ....

Topic 1

p. 36	**motorist** ['məʊtrɪst]	Autofahrer; Autofahrerin
	to **give sb the green light** [ˌɡɪv ˌsʌmbədi ðə ˌɡriːn 'laɪt]	jmdm. grünes Licht geben
	vertical garden [ˌvɜːtɪkl 'ɡɑːdn]	Fassadenbegrünung
	quality ['kwɒləti]	Qualität; Eigenschaft; Merkmal
	level ['levl]	Höhe; Grenze; Niveau
	infrastructure ['ɪnfrəˌstrʌktʃə]	Infrastruktur
	feature ['fiːtʃə]	Merkmal; Bestandteil; Besonderheit; Dokumentarbericht
	architect ['ɑːkɪtekt]	Architekt; Architektin
	environmentally friendly [ɪnˌvaɪrnˌmentli 'frendli]	umweltfreundlich
	scheme [skiːm]	Programm; Plan; Maßnahme; Schema
	concrete ['kɒŋkriːt]	Beton(-)
	column ['kɒləm]	*hier:* Pfeiler; Spalte
	motorway *(BE)* ['məʊtəweɪ]	Autobahn
	to **claim** [kleɪm]	behaupten; beanspruchen
	to **filter** ['fɪltə]	filtern
	harmful ['hɑːmfl]	schädlich
	moreover [mɔːr'əʊvə]	außerdem; ferner; zudem
	in favour of [ɪn 'feɪvər ˌɒv]	für; zugunsten von
	square [skweə]	Quadrat(-); Platz; Spielfeld
	sustainable [sə'steɪnəbl]	nachhaltig
	to **turn out** [ˌtɜːn ˌ'aʊt]	sich herausstellen; sich erweisen
	environmental [ɪnˌvaɪrn'mentl]	Umwelt-
	to **recycle** [ˌriː'saɪkl]	recyceln; wiederverwerten
	sensor ['sensə]	Sensor
	to **ensure** [ɪn'ʃɔː]	sicherstellen; gewährleisten
	to **waste** [weɪst]	verschwenden
	sky-high [ˌskaɪ 'haɪ]	schwindelerregend hoch
	cost [kɒst]	Kosten; Preis
	to **justify** ['dʒʌstɪfaɪ]	rechtfertigen

to **materialise** *(BE)* [mə'tɪərɪəlaɪz]	sich verwirklichen
key [ki:]	wesentlich; Haupt-
factor ['fæktə]	Faktor; Gesichtspunkt; Einfluss
species ['spi:ʃi:z]	Art; Spezies
to **convert** [kən'vɜ:t]	umwandeln
carbon ['kɑ:bn]	Kohlenstoff
oxygen ['ɒksɪdʒən]	Sauerstoff
as a result [əz_ə rɪ'zʌlt]	als Folge
as far as I can see [əz ˌfɑ:r_əz_aɪ kən 'si:]	soweit ich es beurteilen kann
to **encourage** [ɪn'kʌrɪdʒ]	ermutigen; unterstützen
biodiversity [ˌbaɪəʊdaɪ'vɜ:səti]	Artenvielfalt
to **absorb** [əb'zɔ:b]	aufnehmen; absorbieren
heat [hi:t]	Hitze
to **point out** [ˌpɔɪnt_'aʊt]	zeigen; darauf hinweisen
in summary [ɪn 'sʌmri]	zusammenfassend
unless [ən'les]	wenn nicht; außer wenn
to **take** [teɪk]	*hier:* brauchen
p. 38 **smart** [smɑ:t]	*hier:* smart *(mit künstlicher Intelligenz arbeitend)*; schlau; clever; schick
drone [drəʊn]	Drohne
package ['pækɪdʒ]	Paket; Verpackung
fossil fuel ['fɒsl ˌfju:əl]	fossiler Brennstoff
to **dump** [dʌmp]	abladen
landfill site ['lænfɪl ˌsaɪt]	Mülldeponie
eco- ['i:kəʊ]	Öko-
pea [pi:]	Erbse
p. 39 **rubbish bin** *(BE)* ['rʌbɪʃ ˌbɪn]	Abfalleimer
packaging ['pækɪdʒɪŋ]	Verpackung; Verpackungsmaterial
fast fashion [ˌfɑ:st 'fæʃn]	Billigmode *(trendige Mode zu Billigpreisen, die nur kurz getragen und dann wieder weggeworfen wird)*

5 Complete the dialogue.

Juan: Hey Lucy. Have you heard that the v ＿＿＿＿＿＿

g ＿＿＿＿＿＿ project has been g ＿＿＿＿＿＿

t ＿＿ g ＿＿＿＿＿＿ l ＿＿＿＿＿＿ ? I think it's great

that the government is trying to help cities become

more e ＿＿＿＿＿＿＿＿ f ＿＿＿＿＿＿ .

Lucy: Yes, that is good news. Although I'm not sure if it will

solve all of our en ＿＿＿＿＿＿＿＿ problems.

U ＿＿＿＿＿＿ the plants can really convert all of

the h ＿＿＿＿＿ gases, I think it's very difficult to

j ＿＿＿＿＿＿ the scheme. Especially when

the c ＿＿＿＿＿ are so high.

Juan: A ＿＿ f ＿＿＿＿ a ＿ I c ＿＿＿ s ＿＿＿ , it will

definitely make life in cities more s ＿＿＿＿＿＿＿ .

The gardens are built to e ＿＿＿＿＿＿ that no water is

w ＿＿＿＿＿＿ , and I hope that they'll also increase

b ＿＿＿＿＿＿ in the area. And they might

a ＿＿＿＿＿＿ some of the noise of the traffic.

Lucy: That would be good. I'm definitely i ＿＿＿＿

f ＿＿＿＿＿＿ o ＿＿ solutions like this –

I just hope it t ＿＿＿＿＿＿ o ＿＿＿＿ to be as good as

people say.

Juan: Yes, me too.

6 Match the words with their definitions.

1. someone who drives a car	a) cost
2. someone who designs buildings	b) scheme
3. a project/plan/idea	c) key
4. a large road	d) motorist
5. good for the environment	e) sustainable
6. price	f) species
7. main/most important	g) motorway
8. a type of animal or plant	h) architect

7 Write the words in English.

1. _____

2. _____

3. _____

4. _____

8 Find the wrong word.

1. packaging • rubbish bin • landfill site • biodiversity

2. eco- • harmful • sustainable • environmental

3. vertical garden • oil • carbon • fossil fuel

4. encourage • recycle • filter • convert

9 Complete the text.

architects schemes environmental packaging twaste landfill sites ifl sustainable environmentally friendly uencourage censure

Nowadays, new _____ should always be

_____ . For example, when _____

plan new buildings, they should _____ that the

buildings are _____ _____ .

Companies also have a responsibility to try to _____

less so that _____ _____ aren't so

full. A good way to do this is to use less

_____ . The government can also

_____ people to think about

the _____ consequences of their decisions.

Topic 2

p. 44	to **worry** ['wʌri]	hier: beunruhigen
	to **sign** [saɪn]	unterschreiben; unterzeichnen
	petition [pə'tɪʃn]	Petition; Unterschriftenliste
	medication [ˌmedɪ'keɪʃn]	Medikament(e)
	painkiller ['peɪnˌkɪlə]	Schmerzmittel
	production [prə'dʌkʃn]	Produktion; Herstellung
	overall [ˌəʊvr'ɔ:l]	Gesamt-; allgemein
	lorry (BE) ['lɒri]	Lastwagen; Lkw
	by the way [ˌbaɪ ðə 'weɪ]	übrigens
	medical ['medɪkl]	medizinisch; ärztlich
	pandemic [pæn'demɪk]	Seuche; Pandemie
	protection [prə'tekʃn]	Schutz
	if (the) worst comes to (the) worst [ɪf (ðə) ˌwɜːst kʌmz tə (ðə) 'wɜːst]	im schlimmsten Fall
	to **demand** [dɪ'mɑːnd]	verlangen; nachfragen
	necessary ['nesəsri]	nötig; notwendig; erforderlich
	to **sum it all up** [tə ˌsʌm ɪt ɔːl ˈʌp]	um es zusammenzufassen
	damage (no pl) ['dæmɪdʒ]	Schaden; Beschädigung
	to **meet** [miːt]	hier: erfüllen
	fake news [ˌfeɪk 'njuːz]	Fake News (in manipulativer Absicht verbreitete Falschmeldungen)
	source [sɔːs]	Quelle
p. 45	**totally** ['təʊtli]	völlig; total
	antibiotic [ˌæntɪbaɪ'ɒtɪk]	Antibiotikum; antibiotisch
	admin (= administrator) (infml) ['ædmɪn (əd'mɪnɪstreɪtə)]	Admin (Betreuer/-in eines Netzwerks/Computersystems)
	inappropriate [ˌɪnə'prəʊpriət]	unangemessen; ungeeignet
	backward ['bækwəd]	rückständig
	interpretation [ɪnˌtɜːprɪ'teɪʃn]	Interpretation; Auslegung
	trade [treɪd]	Handel; Gewerbe
	contract ['kɒntrækt]	Vertrag

agreement [ə'gri:mənt]	Abkommen; Einigkeit; Zustimmung
healthcare *(no pl)* ['helθkeə]	Gesundheitsversorgung; Gesundheitswesen
definitely ['defɪnətli]	bestimmt; definitiv; eindeutig
Asian ['eɪʒn]	asiatisch; Asiate; Asiatin
manufacture *(no pl)* [ˌmænjə'fæktʃə]	Herstellung; Produktion; Fertigung
according to [ə'kɔ:dɪŋ tə]	laut; gemäß
spelling ['spelɪŋ]	*hier:* Rechtschreib-
swear word ['sweə ˌwɜ:d]	Schimpfwort
to differ ['dɪfə]	sich unterscheiden; abweichen

p. 46	**in case** [ɪn 'keɪs]	für den Fall, dass ...; falls
	therefore ['ðeəfɔ:]	deshalb; deswegen; daher; somit
	to punish ['pʌnɪʃ]	bestrafen
	to take action [ˌteɪk ˈækʃn]	eingreifen; handeln
	ice cap ['aɪs ˌkæp]	Polkappe

10 Complete the sentences.

contract · trade · Asian · meet · medication

1. The _ _ _ _ _ _ _ _ _ _ which we use is often

   produced in other countries.

2. When you get a new job, you have to sign

   a _ _ _ _ _ _ _ _.

3. Some companies do not _ _ _ _ the standards for

   safe working conditions.

4. Lots of products that we buy are made by _ _ _ _ _

   companies.

5. International _ _ _ _ _ is very important for us.

11 Complete the sentences with the right forms of the verbs.

take action   sign   meet   differ   punish   worry

1. Does this product _____ environmental standards?

2. She _____ the petition yesterday.

3. Companies which don't pay their workers enough should be _____ by the government.

4. How much does your new workplace _____ from your old workplace?

5. The government should _____ against companies which treat their workers badly.

6. The amount of pollution in large cities definitely _____ me.

12 Match the opposites.

1. to be the same   a) protection

2. to do nothing   b) inappropriate

3. unnecessary   c) to take action

4. threat   d) necessary

5. acceptable   e) to differ

13 Choose the right word.

The internet is an important _____ (source/
protection) of information, but it can also cause
a lot of _____ (pandemic/damage) if
it is not used correctly. Everyone can share their
opinions on the internet, even if those opinions
are _____ (antibiotic/backward) or offensive.
People can also post _____ (inappropriate/
definitely) pictures and videos. One of the biggest problems
is _____ (overall/fake news). Therefore it
is _____ (necessary/according to) that we are
careful when we read or watch things online.

14 Match the words with their definitions.

1. production   a) antibiotic

2. completely   b) demand

3. a type of medicine   c) backward

4. old-fashioned   d) sign

5. to ask for something   e) lorry

6. something used to transport goods   f) manufacture

7. to write your name on something   g) totally

15 Complete the dialogue.

Rob: Hi, and welcome back to our podcast. Today we're talking about global t _____ and some of the problems in the m_____ industry.

Scarlett: The p_____ of tablets and other medication often takes place in other countries. However, this means that if there is a crisis, for example a p_____, it can be difficult to get the protection that we need. I _____ t_____ w_____ c_____ t_____ t_____ w_____ , people might not be able to get their m_____ . That's why I think it's important to have more local s_____ too.

Rob: I agree. We d_____ need to have more control over our own h_____ system i_____ c_____ there is a crisis. Maybe we could make new agreements with other countries.

Scarlett: Yes. B_____ t_____ w_____ , if you'd like to t_____ a_____ and try to change things, you can s_____ my p_____.
You can find the link on our website.

Text 2

p. 48	**conference** ['kɒnfrns]	Konferenz; Tagung
	effect [ɪ'fekt]	Effekt; Wirkung; Folge
	it's a shame [ˌɪts ə 'ʃeɪm]	schade
	venue ['venju:]	Veranstaltungsort; Treffpunkt
	to hold up [ˌhəʊld ˌ'ʌp]	hochhalten
	placard ['plækɑ:d]	Plakat; Transparent
	to fit [fɪt]	passen
	theme [θi:m]	Thema; Motto
	to have a point [ˌhæv ə 'pɔɪnt]	nicht ganz Unrecht haben
	in person [ɪn 'pɜ:sn]	persönlich
	talk [tɔ:k]	*hier:* Vortrag
	scarcity *(no pl)* ['skeəsəti]	Knappheit
	concept ['kɒnsept]	Vorstellung; Idee; Konzept
	mobility *(no pl)* [mə'bɪləti]	Mobilität
	apart from [ə'pɑ:t frəm]	abgesehen von; außer
	Brazil [brə'zɪl]	Brasilien
	participant [pɑ:'tɪsɪpənt]	Teilnehmer; Teilnehmerin
	cheek [tʃi:k]	Wange; Backe
	after all [ˌɑ:ftər ˌ'ɔ:l]	*hier:* doch; immerhin
	to be supposed to *(+ inf)* [bi sə'pəʊzd tə]	sollen
	to freeze [fri:z]	*hier:* erstarren; gefrieren
	frustrating [frʌs'treɪtɪŋ]	frustrierend
	relieved [rɪ'li:vd]	erleichtert
	technical ['teknɪkl]	*hier:* Technik-
	eventually [ɪ'ventʃuəli]	schließlich; endlich; irgendwann
	to fix [fɪks]	fixieren; befestigen; reparieren
	all in all [ˌɔ:l ɪn ˌ'ɔ:l]	alles in allem; insgesamt
	to smuggle ['smʌgl]	schmuggeln
	to give sb a call [ˌgɪv ˌsʌmbədi ə 'kɔ:l]	jmdn. anrufen
	Best (wishes), [ˌbest ('wɪʃɪz)]	Viele Grüße
p. 49	**annoying** [ə'nɔɪɪŋ]	ärgerlich; lästig
	translation [trænz'leɪʃn]	Übersetzung

Korean [kəˈriːən]	Koreaner; Koreanerin; koreanisch
p. 50 **foreigner** [ˈfɒrɪnə]	Ausländer; Ausländerin
sole [səʊl]	(Schuh-)Sohle

16 Choose the right word.

MAIL

Do you want to find out more about the

_____ (effect/translation) you have on

the climate? Come to our _____ (sole/

conference) next Saturday and listen to _____

(checks/talks) by experts about environmental

_____ (themes/participants) including

_____ (mobility/smuggle), water

_____ (foreigner/security) and sustainable

eating _____ (placards/concepts).

If you have any questions, _____

(give us a call/have a point). Our number is on our

website, where you can also find information about the

_____ (translation/venue).

We look forward to meeting you _____

(in person/relieved) soon!

17 Write the words and find the missing noun.

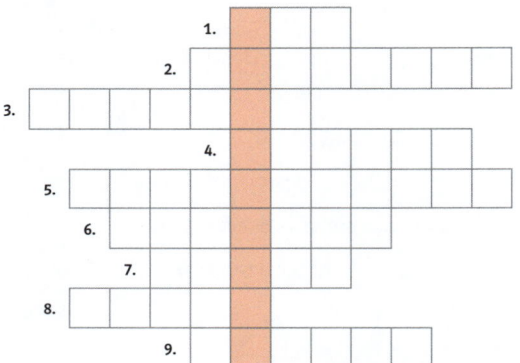

1. If a T-shirt is too large for you, it doesn't … .

2. The ability to move is called … .

3. A sign or poster can also be called a … .

4. Another word for 'impact' is … .

5. Someone who takes part in something is a … .

6. If you bring something into a country illegally, you … it.

7. A … is a place where an event happens.

8. Another word for 'motto' is … .

9. … is a large country in South America.

A _ _ _ _ _ _ _ _ _

is somebody who comes from a different country.

18 Find the wrong word.

1. scarcity • mobility • concept • sole

2. depressing • frustrating • technical • annoying

3. conference • venue • talk • Brazil

4. after all • cheek • all in all • eventually

19 Match the sentence parts.

1. It's a shame   a) I felt very relieved.

2. Social media is useful   b) so I need someone to fix it.

3. His new boyfriend is   c) but there's an English
                                     translation.

4. My uncle lives in   d) that the café was closed.

5. My laptop broke   e) Korean.

6. After the exam,   f) but it's nice to see people
                                     in person too.

7. The book was written   g) Brazil.
   in Russian

If you find some words hard to remember, write them on small pieces of paper and spread them around your room. If you see them again and again, they will be easier to remember.

20 Complete the phone call.

in person   effects   conference   annoying   technical

have a point   after all   all in all   it's a shame

theme   apart   talk   mobility

Meiying: Hi Ryan. How are you? _____
you couldn't come to the 'Green City' _____
last week – you would've loved it!

Ryan: I know, it's really _____ that I
couldn't go. _____, I'm involved in so many
environmental projects so it would've been perfect for me!
What was the _____ this year?

Meiying: It was all about _____. One person gave
a _____ about public transport, and someone
else talked about the _____ of travelling by plane.

Ryan: Well, they _____. I think
lots of people go on holiday abroad too often. What was it like
meeting all the experts _____?

Meiying: Really cool! It was such a great experience,
_____ from the _____ problems,
of course.

Ryan: Oh no, that always happens!

Meiying: I know. But luckily it was fixed quite quickly, and
_____ it was a great day.

Ryan: That's good. I'm looking forward to being there next
year.

Look at literature

p. 58	**vision** ['vɪʒn]	Vision; Vorstellung; Sicht
	professional [prə'feʃnl]	*hier:* beruflich
	financial [faɪ'nænʃl]	finanziell; Finanz-
	idea [aɪ'dɪə]	*hier:* Vorstellung
	far [fɑː]	*hier:* fern
	pill [pɪl]	Pille; Tablette
	to **break free** [ˌbreɪk 'friː]	ausbrechen; sich befreien
	constant ['kɒnstənt]	ständig; konstant; permanent
	to **observe** [əb'zɜːv]	beobachten; beachten; befolgen
	to **be in charge (of)**	das Sagen haben; zuständig
	[biˌ ɪn 'tʃɑːdʒ əv]	sein (für)
	handmaid ['hænmeɪd]	Magd; Dienerin
	tale [teɪl]	Geschichte; Erzählung
	republic [rɪ'pʌblɪk]	Republik
	property ['prɒpəti]	Eigentum; Besitz
	to **handle** ['hændl]	handhaben; umgehen mit
	to **have a baby** [ˌhæv ə 'beɪbi]	ein Kind bekommen
p. 59	**utopian** [juː'təʊpiən]	utopisch
	dystopia [dɪs'təʊpiə]	Dystopie *(negative Utopie)*
	to **reflect** [rɪ'flekt]	spiegeln; reflektieren
	to **criticise** ['krɪtɪsaɪz]	kritisieren
	to **be set (in)** [bi 'set]	spielen
	space [speɪs]	*hier:* Weltraum; Raum; Fläche; Platz
	bad guy ['bæd ˌgaɪ]	Bösewicht; Schurke
	to **occur** [ə'kɜː]	sich ereignen; vorkommen
	fantasy ['fæntəsi]	Fantasie; Fantasy
	magical ['mædʒɪkl]	zauberhaft; magisch
	reality TV [riˈæləti tiːˌviː]	Reality-TV *(Fernsehprogramme, in denen die Wirklichkeit ab-gebildet werden soll)*
	handsome ['hænsəm]	attraktiv; gut aussehend
	judge [dʒʌdʒ]	Juror; Jurorin; Richter; Richterin
	flawed [flɔːd]	fehlerhaft; mangelhaft
	moral ['mɒrl]	moralisch

L

	ethical ['eθɪkl]	ethisch; moralisch
	to **mark** [ma:k]	markieren; kennzeichnen
	to **question** ['kwestʃən]	befragen; bezweifeln
p. 65	to **touch** [tʌtʃ]	berühren
	to **back up** [ˌbæk ˈʌp]	*hier:* unterstützen; Daten sichern
p. 66	to **get in trouble** [ˌget ɪn ˈtrʌbl]	Schwierigkeiten bekommen

1 Complete the sentences and find the answer to 8.

1. The prince in the story was very __ __ __ [ ] __ __ __ __ .

2. 'The Lord of the Rings' is a __ __ __ __ __ __ [ ] series.

3. The film shows a very negative __ __ [ ] __ __ __ of the future.

4. Lots of people like __ __ __ __ __ [ ] TV.

5. Some authors write books which ask __ [ ] __ __ __ questions.

6. A __ __ __ [ ] __ __ __ society is a society which is perfect.

7. It is very difficult to become a __ __ __ __ __ __ __ [ ] __ __ __ author.

8. Another word for 'story' is '__ [ ] __ __ .'

[ ] [ ] [ ] [ ] [ ] [ ] [ ]

2 **Complete the sentences with the right forms of the verbs.**

reflect   break free   handle   criticise   question

be set in   be in charge of   get in trouble

1. The prisoner tried to _____ last night.

2. His brother _____ our football team.

3. They _____ the situation very well yesterday.

4. The book _____ many of the problems of

   modern society.

5. The film was _____ by some people because it

   was too violent.

6. She likes books which _____ the past.

7. In this book, the author _____ whether society is

   really free.

8. She _____ at school yesterday because

   she didn't do her homework.

3 **Complete the summary of the novel.**

Celestine lives in a society which m_____ people who

are 'f_____' – that means they have done something

wrong. At the start, she doesn't c_____ the system,

but then something o_____ on the bus which makes

her realise some of the e_____ problems of the

society she lives in. This makes her q_____ her beliefs.

L

4 Complete the text.

the space hfgdystopiangfrobservedhaconstantjuzc riticisewamoralefideaght

There are lots of different types of _____ novels,

but all of them show a very negative _____ of what

the future will be like. Some show societies where people are

in _____ danger, for example because of war

or disease. Others show societies where people are always

being _____ by the government. Sometimes

the stories include aspects of science fiction, like creatures

or technology from _____. There are often

difficult _____ choices which the characters have to

make. The authors of these novels are usually trying to

_____ something about modern society.

5 Match the words with their definitions.

1. something which you own
2. to do with money
3. a type of government
4. the opposite of the hero
5. to support or agree with someone
6. the opposite of near
7. to put your hand on somebody or something

a) republic
b) bad guy
c) far
d) touch
e) property
f) back up
g) financial

Unit 3 International work and trade

Intro

<table>
<tr><td>p. 68</td><td>banking ['bæŋkɪŋ]</td><td>Bankwesen; Bankgeschäft; Bank-</td></tr>
<tr><td></td><td>boomtown ['buːmtaʊn]</td><td>Boomtown (eine Stadt, die sehr schnell wächst)</td></tr>
<tr><td></td><td>cost of living [ˌkɒst‿əv 'lɪvɪŋ]</td><td>Lebenshaltungskosten</td></tr>
<tr><td></td><td>freelance ['friːlɑːns]</td><td>Freiberufler; Freiberuflerin; freiberuflich</td></tr>
<tr><td></td><td>translator [trænz'leɪtə]</td><td>Übersetzer; Übersetzerin</td></tr>
<tr><td></td><td>the Bahamas [ðə bə'hɑːməz]</td><td>die Bahamas (Inselgruppe in der Karibik)</td></tr>
<tr><td></td><td>a number of [ə 'nʌmbər‿əv]</td><td>einige; mehrere</td></tr>
<tr><td></td><td>to interest ['ɪntrəst]</td><td>interessieren</td></tr>
<tr><td></td><td>for good [fə 'ɡʊd]</td><td>für immer; endgültig</td></tr>
<tr><td>p. 69</td><td>to move in with sb [ˌmuːv‿ɪn‿wɪð]</td><td>mit jmdm. zusammenziehen</td></tr>
<tr><td></td><td>course [kɔːs]</td><td>Kurs</td></tr>
<tr><td></td><td>accounting [ə'kaʊntɪŋ]</td><td>Buchführung; Buchhaltung</td></tr>
<tr><td></td><td>Syria ['sɪriə]</td><td>Syrien</td></tr>
<tr><td></td><td>parcel ['pɑːsl]</td><td>Paket; Päckchen</td></tr>
<tr><td></td><td>grateful ['ɡreɪtfl]</td><td>dankbar</td></tr>
<tr><td></td><td>sick pay ['sɪk ˌpeɪ]</td><td>Krankengeld</td></tr>
<tr><td></td><td>to be made redundant [biː ˌmeɪd rɪ'dʌndənt]</td><td>den Arbeitsplatz verlieren</td></tr>
<tr><td></td><td>to outsource ['aʊtsɔːs]</td><td>auslagern; outsourcen</td></tr>
<tr><td></td><td>devastated ['devəsteɪtɪd]</td><td>niedergeschmettert</td></tr>
<tr><td></td><td>to be on the dole (infml) [bi‿ɒn ðə 'dəʊl]</td><td>Arbeitslosengeld bekommen</td></tr>
</table>

There are lots of different apps that can help you to practise your vocabulary. Have you tried them yet?

1 Complete the texts.

INTERNET

The Student Job Forum

Hi, my name's Hwan and I'd like to become

a t_____. I can already speak a

n_____ o_____ languages and I would love to

do f_____ work for companies in lots of

different countries.

(Hwan, 18)

I'm Lizzy and I'm looking for a job in b_____.

There are lots of opportunities in London but the

c_____ o____ l_____ there is so high. I'm

hoping I can m_____ i____ w_____

a friend until I find work and a place to live.

(Lizzy, 19)

My name's Nadiya. I've been working as a waitress but

I w_____ m_____ r_____

last month. Of course I was d_____ at

first, but now I've found an online c_____ in

a_____ which really i_____ me.

(Nadiya, 19)

2 Find the words.

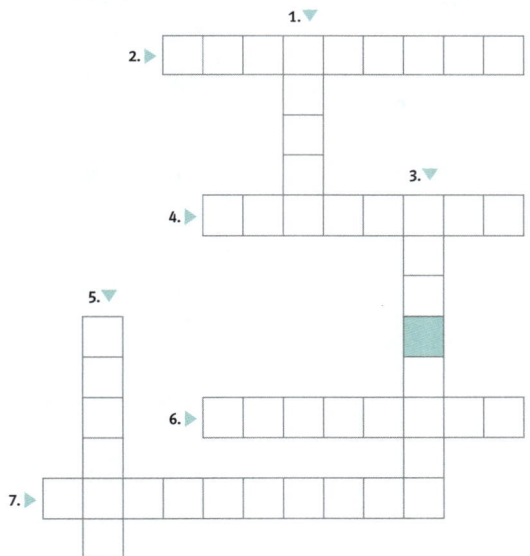

1. a country in Asia
  3. forever
  5. a package that is sent
     by post

▶ 2. when a company pays
     another company to do
     parts of its work
  4. thankful
  6. a city which is growing
     very fast
  7. very unhappy

3

Topic 1

dialect [ˈdaɪəlekt] — Dialekt

Cantonese [ˌkæntəˈniːz] — Kantonesisch; kantonesisch

density [ˈdensɪti] — Dichte

UTC (= Coordinated Universal Time) [ˌjuːtiːˈsiː] — (koordinierte) Weltzeit

to **hand back** [ˌhænd ˈbæk] — zurückgeben

SAR (= special administrative region) [ˌeseɪˈɑː] — Sonderverwaltungszone

tax [tæks] — Steuer

customs duty [ˈkʌstəmz ˌdjuːti] — Zollabgabe

to **import** [ɪmˈpɔːt] — importieren; einführen

image [ˈɪmɪdʒ] — hier: Image; Bild

position [pəˈzɪʃn] — hier: Stellung; Position; Stelle

gateway [ˈɡeɪtweɪ] — Tor; Eingangstor

to **turn into** [ˌtɜːnˌˈɪntə] — umwandeln in; verwandeln in

port [pɔːt] — Hafen

major [ˈmeɪdʒə] — Haupt-; wichtig; bedeutend

dense [dens] — dicht

populated [ˈpɒpjəleɪtɪd] — bevölkert; besiedelt

consequently [ˈkɒnsɪkwəntli] — folglich; somit

upwards [ˈʌpwədz] — aufwärts; nach oben

side effect [ˈsaɪd ɪˌfekt] — Nebenwirkung

life expectancy [ˈlaɪf ɪkˌspektnsi] — Lebenserwartung

range [reɪndʒ] — Reihe; Auswahl

to **relax** [rɪˈlæks] — sich entspannen

harmony [ˈhɑːməni] — Harmonie; Eintracht

to **fly** [flaɪ] — hier: wehen lassen; hissen

governmental [ˌɡʌvnˈmentl] — Regierungs-; staatlich

legal [ˈliːɡl] — legal; rechtlich; Rechts-

stall [stɔːl] — Stand; Bude

to **swap** [swɒp] — tauschen

addict [ˈædɪkt] — Süchtiger; Süchtige

latest [ˈleɪtɪst] — neueste

out [aʊt] — hier: erhältlich

to **browse** [braʊz] — durchstöbern

discount ['dɪskaʊnt]		Rabatt; Preisnachlass
p. 72 to **hug** [hʌg]		umarmen
chilly ['tʃɪli]		kühl
headphones *(pl)* ['hedfəʊnz]		Kopfhörer
luggage ['lʌgɪdʒ]		Gepäck
to **take off** [ˌteɪk ˈɒf]		*hier:* abheben
toy [tɔɪ]		Spielzeug(-)
arrival [əˈraɪvl]		Ankunft
noodle ['nu:dl]		Nudel
hectic ['hektɪk]		hektisch
mass transit *(AE)*		öffentlicher Nahverkehr;
[ˌmæs ˈtrænsɪt]		Massen-
to **pay attention to sth**		seine Aufmerksamkeit
[ˌpeɪ əˈtenʃn]		auf etw. richten
to **run over** [ˌrʌn ˈəʊvə]		überfahren
to **pull over** [ˌpʊl ˈəʊvə]		zur Seite fahren
to **get out** [ˌget ˈaʊt]		herauskommen; aussteigen
for ages [fər ˈeɪdʒɪz]		ewig lange

3   Put the words into the table.

density   relax   browse   major   populated

swap   arrival   dense   port

Nouns	Verbs	Adjectives

4 Complete the newspaper article.

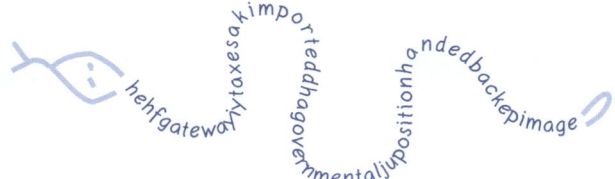

hehfgatewaiytaxesakimporteddhagovernmentaljupositionhandedbackepimage

---

Evening News

Hong Kong: A global power

Hong Kong has earned its _____ as an

important global financial centre. The _____

there are low and there are also no customs duties on

products which are _____ or exported.

This means that Hong Kong has an important

_____ in the global economy as a

_____ between China and other countries

like the USA.

Its political situation is unique because it is part of China

but it still has its own _____

system. It was _____

to China in 1997 after many years of British influence.

---

5 Complete the text.

Chinese and English are the two official languages in Hong

Kong. Most people who live there speak C_____ ,

which is a d_____ . Hong Kong is very

d_____ because so many people live there.

C_____ , many buildings have been built

u_____ , since there isn't room on the ground for

all the people. Hong Kong plays a m_____ role in

international trade, but it also offers a r_____ of

amazing sights. Tourists can r_____ in the beautiful

parks and b_____ for souvenirs at the street markets.

6 Complete the sentences with the right words.

| into | over | off | over | out |

1. She pulled the car _____ to look at the map.

2. These old office buildings will be turned _____ flats.

3. Be careful not to get run _____ by a car.

4. Once we had arrived, we all got _____ of the car.

5. Our flight took _____ at eight o'clock in the evening.

7 Write the words in English.

1. _____

2. _____

3. _____

8 Find the words and match them with their definitions.

a) Find seven words.

N	H	R	Y	L	E	G	A	L	T
A	E	I	M	P	O	R	T	U	C
R	C	E	H	B	Q	L	I	G	H
E	T	O	Y	R	S	V	U	G	I
H	I	S	C	N	X	I	K	A	L
D	C	E	W	U	A	R	L	G	L
H	A	R	M	O	N	Y	N	E	Y

b) Write the words next to the right definitions.

1. something that children play with: _____

2. a bit cold: _____

3. peace: _____

4. to do with law: _____

5. what you bring with you when you travel somewhere:

   _____

6. to bring something into a country from another country:

   _____

7. very busy: _____

Topic 2

p. 76	**thread** [θred]	Zwirn; Garn; Faden
	ever-shorter [ˌevə ˈʃɔːtə]	immer kürzer (werdend)
	toxic [ˈtɒksɪk]	giftig; toxisch
	chemical [ˈkemɪkl]	Chemikalie; chemisch
	unsafe [ʌnˈseɪf]	unsicher; gefährlich
	working conditions (pl only) [ˈwɜːkɪŋ kənˌdɪʃnz]	Arbeitsbedingungen
	to **stitch** [stɪtʃ]	sticken; nähen
	to **rethink** [ˌriːˈθɪŋk]	überdenken; überlegen
	to **launch** [lɔːnʃ]	einführen; starten; abschießen
	cupboard [ˈkʌbəd]	Schrank
	to **refashion** [ˌriːˈfæʃn]	*aus Altkleidern modische Kleidung machen*
	to **donate** [dəˈneɪt]	spenden; stiften
	trained [treɪnd]	ausgebildet
	tights (pl) [taɪts]	Strumpfhose
	to **upcycle** [ʌpˈsaɪkl]	upcyceln *(Wiederverwertung von Abfallstoffen)*
	cushion [ˈkʊʃn]	Kissen; Polster
	coat [kəʊt]	Mantel; Jacke
	jumper *(BE)* [ˈdʒʌmpə]	Pullover; Pulli
	thrilled [θrɪld]	außer sich vor Freude; sehr erfreut
	donation [dəˈneɪʃn]	Spende; Schenkung
	to **compress** [kəmˈpres]	komprimieren; zusammenpressen
	textile [ˈtekstaɪl]	textil; Textil-
	filling [ˈfɪlɪŋ]	*hier:* Futter
	mattress [ˈmætrəs]	Matratze
	vegan [ˈviːgən]	Veganer; Veganerin; vegan
	fabric [ˈfæbrɪk]	Stoff
	organic [ɔːˈgænɪk]	Bio-; organisch
	cotton [ˈkɒtn]	Baumwolle
	linen *(no pl)* [ˈlɪnɪn]	Leinen(-)
	bamboo [bæmˈbuː]	Bambus

polyester [ˌpɒliˈestə]	Polyester
to **rent** [rent]	mieten
instead of [ɪnˈsted‿əv]	statt; anstatt; anstelle von
p. 77 **shorts** *(pl)* [ʃɔːts]	Shorts; kurze Hose
to **match** [mætʃ]	*hier:* passen (zu)
greenhouse gas emissions	Ausstoß von Treibhausgasen
[ˌgriːnhaʊs ˈgæs‿iˌmɪʃnz]	
microplastics *(pl)*	Mikroplastik
[ˌmaɪkrəʊˈplæstɪks]	
fibre [ˈfaɪbə]	Faser
waste [weɪst]	*hier:* Verschwendung
urgent [ˈɜːdʒnt]	dringend
renewable [rɪˈnjuːəbl]	erneuerbar; verlängerbar
rather than [ˈrɑːðə ðən]	als; eher als
p. 78 **complaint** [kəmˈpleɪnt]	Beschwerde
Dear Sir or Madam,	Sehr geehrte Damen und
[dɪə ˌsɜːr‿ɔː ˈmædəm]	Herren,
medium [ˈmiːdiəm]	mittel(groß)
confirmation [ˌkɒnfəˈmeɪʃn]	Bestätigung(s-)
within [wɪˈðɪn]	innerhalb
apology [əˈpɒlədʒi]	Entschuldigung
order [ˈɔːdə]	*hier:* Bestellung; Reihenfolge
to **look into** [ˌlʊk ˈɪntu]	untersuchen; überprüfen
delay [dɪˈleɪ]	Verzögerung; Verspätung
refund [ˈriːfʌnd]	Rückerstattung
otherwise [ˈʌðəwaɪz]	sonst
supervisor [ˈsuːpəvaɪzə]	Vorgesetzter; Vorgesetzte
to **appreciate** [əˈpriːʃieɪt]	schätzen; anerkennen
to **get back to sb** [ˌget ˈbæk tʊ]	sich wieder bei jmdm. melden
Yours faithfully, [ˌjɔːz ˈfeɪθfli]	Mit freundlichen Grüßen
p. 79 **label** [ˈleɪbl]	Markenname; Etikett; Beschriftung
to **unsubscribe** [ˌʌnsəbˈskraɪb]	sich abmelden; abbestellen
branded [ˈbrændɪd]	Marken-
fake [feɪk]	künstlich; gefälscht

9 Complete the e-mails.

MAIL

Dear Sir or Madam,

I am writing because I have a c_____ about

a T-shirt which I ordered from your company. I made

the o_____ online at the start of the month

and it arrived three weeks late. It was also the wrong size

and colour. Therefore I would like a r_____

w_____ a week.

My customer reference number is: G65DFAI826

Y_____ f_____,

Amelia Grey

MAIL

Dear Ms Grey,

Please accept my a_____ that you received the

wrong o_____. I will speak to my s_____

about your c_____ and she will

l_____ i_____ the problem to make sure it

doesn't happen again. Please g_____ b_____

t_____ m_____ if the money doesn't arrive

w_____ five days.

Yours sincerely,

Leon Hunt

---

10 Write the words in English.

1. _____

2. _____

3. _____

4. _____

5. _____

6. _____

7. _____

8. _____

11 Find the wrong word.

1. tights • jumper • thread • coat

2. chemical • cotton • linen • bamboo

3. renewable • urgent • vegan • organic

4. fabric • confirmation • apology • complaint

12 Find five nouns.

1. s __ p __ r v __ s __ r

2. c __ n f __ r m __ t __ __ n

3. c __ t t __ n

4. d __ n __ t __ __ n

5. f __ b r __ c

13 Put the adjectives into the right sentences.

toxic   unsafe   trained   thrilled   vegan   organic

renewable   urgent

1. She was _____ when she found out that

   she had got the job.

2. Lots of countries are trying to use more

   _____ energy sources.

3. We only buy _____ meat and eggs.

4. The restaurant offers a lot of _____ food.

5. That bridge looks very _____ .

6. The factory produces a lot of _____ waste.

7. All of our employees are _____ in either

   banking or accounting.

8. Can I talk to you for a moment? It's _____ !

14 Match the words with their definitions.

1. dangerous   a) renewable

2. what the workplace is like   b) delay

3. to start or introduce something   c) launch

4. when you say you are sorry   d) unsafe

5. when something is late   e) apologise

6. something which you can   f) working conditions
   use again and again

15 Choose the right word.

Lots of companies in the fashion industry are

starting to _____ (donate/rethink)

how they make their products. Climate change is

an _____ (urgent/organic) problem which needs

solutions, and the fashion industry can help to reduce waste

and _____ (greenhouse

gas emissions/shorts).

Some companies have started to _____

(match/refashion) old clothes – for example, if someone

_____ (launches/donates) an old

_____ (jumper/tights), the designers at the

company can use it to make a _____

(donation/cushion).

Companies can also _____ (compress/look

into) old materials which can't be used for clothes anymore

and use them to make _____ (microplastics/

filling) for _____ (mattresses/bamboo).

So next time you have some clothes you don't want anymore,

think about making a _____ (textile/

donation) to a sustainable fashion company of your choice

_____ (instead of/within) just throwing them

away.

16 Complete the dialogue.

James: Alex, have you bought a dress to wear to Zac's party on Friday?

Alex: I think I'm going to r_____ a dress i_____ o_____ buying one. There's a new sustainable clothes shop in town where people can d_____ their old things, and there are also highly- t_____ designers who make new clothes from o_____ materials.

James: That's such a good idea!

Alex: Yes, it was only l_____ two weeks ago so I haven't been there yet, but I've heard it's really cool.

James: Yeah, I think that's great. Lots of clothes factories produce c_____ which damage the environment, and lots of the m_____ in the oceans also come from clothes.

Alex: Exactly. And sometimes the clothes we buy are produced in factories which are u_____ and have bad w_____ c_____. That's why I want to support sustainable fashion projects like this one. I've already found the perfect dress on their website!

James: Nice, do you have a photo?

Alex: Sure, here it is. It m_____ my shoes perfectly.

James: Wow, that looks amazing!

Text 2

p. 80	**alarm** [əˈlaːm]	Alarm(anlage); Beunruhigung
	to **board** [bɔːd]	an Bord gehen
	deck [dek]	Schiffsdeck
	shipping container [ˈʃɪpɪŋ kənˌteɪnə]	Schiffscontainer
	cargo [ˈkaːgəʊ]	Ladung; Fracht
	bound (for) [ˈbaʊnd (fə)]	unterwegs (nach)
	pitch [pɪtʃ]	Spielfeld; Platz
	officer [ˈɒfɪsə]	*hier:* Offizier; Offizierin
	jumbo jet [ˌdʒʌmbəʊ ˈdʒet]	Jumbojet *(Großraumflugzeug)*
	afloat [əˈfləʊt]	über Wasser
	Malta [ˈmɔːltə]	Malta
	cabin [ˈkæbɪn]	*hier:* Kabine
	to **put up** [ˌpʊtˈʌp]	*hier:* aufhängen
	to **keep track of** [ˌkiːp ˈtræk əv]	im Auge behalten
	progress *(no pl)* [ˈprəʊgres]	Fortschritt
	rather [ˈraːðə]	ziemlich; eher
	little [ˈlɪtl]	*hier:* wenig; kaum
	to **exist** [ɪgˈzɪst]	existieren; bestehen
	Panama [ˈpænəmaː]	Panama
	to **register** [ˈredʒɪstə]	sich registrieren lassen; sich eintragen; sich anmelden
	on board [ˌɒn ˈbɔːd]	an Bord
	Filipino [ˌfɪlɪˈpiːnəʊ]	Filipino *(Bewohner der Philippinen)*; Filipina *(Bewohnerin der Philippinen)*; philippinisch
	curry [ˈkʌri]	Curry *(Gewürz oder Gericht)*
	Malaysian [məˈleɪziən]	Malaysier; Malaysierin; malaysisch
	to **get involved (in)** [ˌget ɪnˈvɒlvd (ɪn)]	sich beteiligen (an); sich engagieren (für); sich einlassen (auf)
	to **admit** [ədˈmɪt]	zugeben; hereinlassen
	naive [naɪˈiːv]	naiv; einfältig

to **sign up** [ˌsaɪnˈʌp]		sich verpflichten; sich einschreiben
to **unload** [ʌnˈləʊd]		entladen; abladen
rare [reə]		rar; selten
p. 81	**piercing** [ˈpɪəsɪŋ]	durchdringend
	fire drill [ˈfaɪə ˌdrɪl]	Feueralarmübung
	to **steer** [stɪə]	steuern; lenken
	sunset [ˈsʌnset]	Sonnenuntergang
	to **flash** [flæʃ]	blitzen; blinken
	pirate [ˈpaɪrət]	Seeräuber; Seeräuberin; Pirat; Piratin
	to **spot** [spɒt]	sehen; erkennen
	to **radio** [ˈreɪdiəʊ]	funken
	shipping route [ˈʃɪpɪŋ ˌruːt]	Schifffahrtsweg
	risk [rɪsk]	Risiko
	chest [tʃest]	Brust(korb)
p. 82	**speedboat** [ˈspiːdbəʊt]	Schnellboot

17 Match the words with their definitions.

1. to get on a plane or boat   a) steer

2. to say that something is true   b) flash

3. to take part in an activity   c) board

4. to see something   d) get involved

5. to control a boat or car   e) spot

6. to shine brightly for a short time   f) admit

18 **Write the words in English.**

1. _____

2. _____

3. _____

4. _____

19 **Complete the newspaper report.**

Evening News

Ships in danger?

A ship b_____ f_____ Shanghai was almost

attacked by p_____ yesterday evening. Luckily

an o_____ sp_____ them in time

and r_____ for help. There are 22 crew members

o_____ b_____ and the ship is carrying

s_____ c_____ filled with

c_____ which will be delivered in Shanghai. The

shipping r_____ is one of the busiest in the world

and the r_____ of being attacked is higher there than

in most areas. However, authorities on land

will k_____ t_____ o_____ the ship's

p_____ until it reaches Shanghai to make

sure it is safe.

20 Find the words.

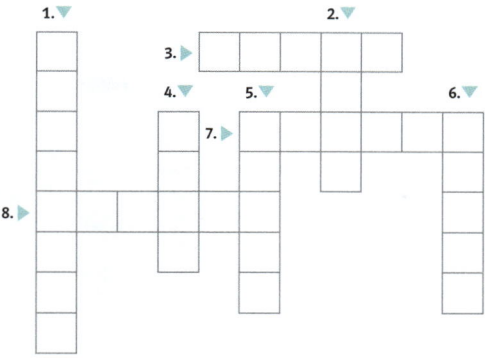

▼ 1. You sometimes have to ... online before you can go to an event.
2. Something which doesn't happen very often is ....
4. When something could be dangerous, there is a ....
5. You play football on a football ....
6. Another word for 'to be' or 'to live' is 'to...'.

▶ 3. When you get on a ship, you ... it.
7. Someone who attacks ships is a ....
8. ... is when the sun goes down.

3

21 Complete the postcard.

Dear Zara,

I hope you're having a good holiday. I'm writing this letter in

my c_____ on the ship which is taking us to Malta.

We b_____ two days ago. Last night I stood on

the d_____ and watched the s_____.

It was beautiful and I even s_____ some fish in the

sea. There are lots of other tourists o____ b_____

and they're all really friendly. I even met a M_____

family who are staying in the same hotel as me when we arrive!

The food is also great – we had a delicious c_____

for lunch today. I have to a_____, I didn't think

I would enjoy living on a ship so much. I hope the hotel is

just as nice!

See you soon,

Heidi

Unit 4 Kia ora, New Zealand!

Intro

p. 90	**literally** ['lɪtrli]	buchstäblich
	stopover ['stɒpˌəʊvə]	Zwischenlandung; Zwischenaufenthalt
	to **get over sth** [ˌgetˌ'əʊvə]	über etw. hinwegkommen; mit etw. fertigwerden
	jet lag ['dʒet ˌlæg]	Jetlag *(Störung des Biorhythmus nach einer weiten Flugreise)*
	earthquake ['ɜːθkweɪk]	Erdbeben
	Maori ['maʊri]	Maori(-); maorisch
	indigenous people [ɪnˌdɪdʒɪnəs 'piːpl]	einheimisches Volk; Ureinwohner; Ureinwohnerinnen
	TV station [ˌtiːviː 'steɪʃn]	Fernsehsender
p. 91	**New Zealander** [ˌnjuː 'ziːləndə]	Neuseeländer; Neuseeländerin
	topic ['tɒpɪk]	Thema
	to **get stranded** [ˌget 'strændɪd]	stranden
	adrenalin(e) junkie [əˈdrenlɪn ˌdʒʌŋki]	Adrenalinjunkie
	enthusiast [ɪnˈθjuːziæst]	Enthusiast; Enthusiastin
	to **flow** [fləʊ]	fließen; strömen
	rugged ['rʌgɪd]	rau; wild
	abseiling ['æbseɪlɪŋ]	Abseilen
	to **head** ['hed]	zusteuern; sich auf den Weg machen
	to **be made up of** [biː ˌmeɪdˌ'ʌpˌəv]	bestehen aus
	approximately [əˈprɒksɪmətli]	ungefähr; etwa
	fjord [fjɔːd]	Fjord
	subtropical [sʌb'trɒpɪkl]	subtropisch
p. 90	**filmmaker** ['fɪlmˌmeɪkə]	Filmemacher; Filmemacherin
p. 91	to **rescue** ['reskjuː]	retten

volunteer [ˌvɒlənˈtɪə]	Freiwilliger; Freiwillige; ehrenamtlicher Helfer; ehrenamtliche Helferin
to **keep away** [ˌkiːp ə'weɪ]	(sich) fernhalten
tail [teɪl]	*hier:* Schwanzflosse; Schwanz; Schweif

1 Complete the text.

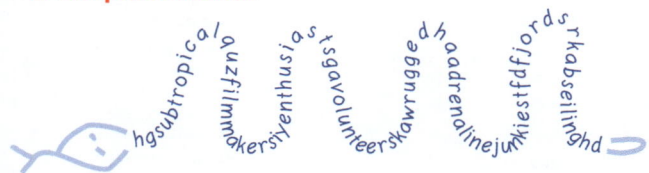

There are lots of reasons why people travel to New Zealand.

For hiking _____ it's the perfect place

to explore nature, and there are lots of beautiful

_____ and even _____ forests.

The _____ landscape is so impressive that

it has also attracted _____, including

Peter Jackson, the director of the fim trilogy 'The Lord

of the Rings'. Queenstown is a popular destination

for _____ _____ as it offers

activities such as bungee-jumping and _____.

Many young people people travel to New Zealand to work

as _____, which is a great way to learn new

skills and experience a different culture.

2 Write the words in English.

1. _____

2. _____

3. _____

4. _____

3 Complete the sentences and find the answer to 9.

1. If you're a film e_ _ _ _ _ ☐_ _ _ _ , you should visit Hobbiton.

2. Our hotel was l_☐_ _ _ _ _ _ right next to the airport.

3. The M_☐_ _ language is now taught in many schools in New Zealand.

4. Climate change is an important t_☐_ _ for many young people.

5. A flight from Germany to New Zealand takes

   a_ _ _ ☐_ _ _ _ _ _ _ _ 24 hours.

6. New Zealand has a Maori T☐ s_ _ _ _ _☐_ .

7. On the first day of the holiday, we h_☐_ _ _ to the South Island.

8. Serious e_☐_ _ _ _ _ _ _ _ can sometimes happen in New Zealand.

9. When we flew to New Zealand, there was a

   ☐☐☐☐☐☐☐☐ in Singapore.

4

Topic 1

p. 92 **if it wasn't for sb**   ohne jmdn.
[ɪfˌɪtˈwɒznt fə]

kiwi [ˈkiːwiː]   Neuseeländer; Neuseeländerin;
Kiwi *(Frucht oder Laufvogel)*

false [fɔːls]   falsch

in the first place   in erster Linie
[ɪn ðə ˈfɜːst ˌpleɪs]

yet [jet]   doch; und trotzdem

disciplined [ˈdɪsəplɪnd]   diszipliniert

traffic light [ˈtræfɪk ˌlaɪt]   (Verkehrs-)Ampel

sense of humour   Sinn für Humor
[ˌsensˌəv ˈhjuːmə]

gnome [nəʊm]   Gnom; Zwerg

honestly [ˈɒnɪstli]   ehrlich

chaotic [keɪˈɒtɪk]   chaotisch

dos and don'ts   Verhaltensregeln
[ˌduːzˌən ˈdəʊnts]

above all [əˌbʌvˈɔːl]   vor allen Dingen; in erster Linie

to **assume** [əˈsjuːm]   annehmen; voraussetzen

to **crack jokes** [ˌkræk ˈdʒəʊks]   Witze reißen

consumer [kənˈsjuːmə]   Konsument; Konsumentin;
Verbraucher; Verbraucherin

to **stick to sth** [ˈstɪk tə]   sich an etw. halten

inhabited [ɪnˈhæbɪtɪd]   bewohnt

humorous [ˈhjuːmrəs]   humorvoll; lustig

plus [plʌs]   *hier:* darüber hinaus; plus

pure [pjʊə]   rein; pur

brochure [ˈbrəʊʃə]   Broschüre; Prospekt

footprint [ˈfʊtprɪnt]   Fußabdruck

rainforest [ˈreɪnˌfɒrɪst]   Regenwald

glow-worm [ˈgləʊwɜːm]   Glühwürmchen

to **light up** [ˌlaɪtˈʌp]   (sich) erhellen; anzünden

to **thunder** [ˈθʌndə]   donnern

p. 93 **ice axe** [ˈaɪsˌæks]   Eispickel

telescope [ˈtelɪskəʊp]   Teleskop; Fernrohr

(a pair of) binoculars *(pl)* [(ə ˌpeər ˌəv) bɪˈnɒkjələz]		(ein) Fernglas
breathtaking [ˈbreθˌteɪkɪŋ]		atemberaubend
to **convince** [kənˈvɪns]		überzeugen
unsurprisingly [ˌʌnsəˈpraɪzɪŋli]		wie nicht anders erwartet
p. 94 **scenic** [ˈsiːnɪk]		landschaftlich (schön)
peace and quiet [ˌpiːs ən ˈkwaɪət]		Ruhe und Frieden
to **consider** [kənˈsɪdə]		betrachten; erwägen
guardian [ˈgɑːdiən]		Hüter; Hüterin; Wächter; Wächterin
inactive [ɪnˈæktɪv]		untätig; inaktiv; passiv
solar energy [ˌsəʊlər ˈenədʒi]		Solarenergie; Sonnenenergie
to **generate** [ˈdʒenəreɪt]		generieren; erzeugen
p. 95 **trilogy** [ˈtrɪlədʒi]		Trilogie
admission fee [ədˈmɪʃn ˌfiː]		Eintritt(spreis)
setting [ˈsetɪŋ]		Schauplatz

4 Match the words with their definitions.

1. wrong, not true

2. funny

3. a series of three

4. most importantly

5. create or make

6. a person who protects something or someone

7. the person who buys or uses a product

a) consumer

b) above all

c) trilogy

d) false

e) guardian

f) humorous

g) generate

5 Complete the text.

Discover New Zealand

This b _____ tells you everything you need to
know about New Zealand's br _____ scenery.
The country is famous for its impressive
landscapes, y _____ many tourists spend most of their
time in cities like Queenstown. But if you want a bit
of p _____ a _____ q _____ , here are some
tips for where to experience the pure natural beauty of New
Zealand.

Firstly, you should go to see one of the r _____.
There are so many amazing animals that live there, although
uns _____ it sometimes rains very
heavily so don't forget your coat!

You could also c _____ going to Lake Tekapo.
It's sc _____ during the day, but at night you can
bring your t _____ or b _____
and look at the stars. Waitomo Caves are also a popular
destination because there are gl _____ which
l _____ u _____ the caves. P _____
you can learn about the science and history behind the caves.

A _____ a _____ , it's important to respect these
natural places, so remember: leave
only f _____.

6 Write the words in English.

1. _____

2. _____

3. _____

4. _____

7 Complete the sentences with the right forms of the verbs.

convince   stick to   crack jokes   assume

generate   consider

1. Please _____ the rules about food and drink while you are in the museum.

2. Last night she _____ me to watch a scary film.

3. At the moment we are _____ whether we should go on holiday to New Zealand this summer.

4. When I'm sad, my dad always _____ to cheer me up.

5. I am sure that in the future, more electricity will be _____ by renewable sources.

6. My mum always _____ that everyone agrees with her holiday plans.

8 Complete the chat.

Sam: Hey Jonas, how's your holiday going? _H_____ ,
I'm so jealous that you're in New Zealand!

Jonas: Hi Sam, it's amazing! Tomorrow we're going to
Hobbiton, which is the main reason why I wanted to go to New
Zealand i__ t_____ f_____ p_____.
'The Lord of the Rings' is such a great film t_____.

Sam: Oh yeah, of course! And have you met many New
Zealanders?

Jonas: Yes, I've spoken to a few people at the hotel and they
all have a great _s_____ of h_____ and are really
helpful. They told us about lots of different _s_____ places
to go and see. And we also had a funny conversation about
stereotypes!

Sam: Oh really? What did they say about German people then?

Jonas: Well, they thought that everyone in Germany
was very _d_____ – for example, one
guy said that Germans never cross the road when
the _t_____ l_____ is red.

Sam: Oops, I do that all the time!

Jonas: I know... And they also _a_____ that everyone
was very organised, but I think they know that's not true now
they've met my _c_____ family!

Sam: Haha, well at least they know the truth now…

Topic 2

p. 98

head first [ˌhed ˈfɜːst]	kopfüber
the unknown [ðiˌʌnˈnəʊn]	das Unbekannte
once-in-a-lifetime [ˌwʌnsˌɪnˌə ˈlaɪftaɪm]	einmalig; einmal im Leben
to **have the time of your life** [hæv ðə ˌtaɪmˌəv jə ˈlaɪf]	sich königlich amüsieren
canyoning *(no pl)* [ˈkænjənɪŋ]	Schluchtenwandern
whitewater rafting [ˌwaɪtwɔːtə ˈrɑːftɪŋ]	Rafting *(Wildwasserfahren)*
bungee jumping [ˈbʌndʒi ˌdʒʌmpɪŋ]	Bungee-Jumping
a length of elastic cord [əˌleŋθˌəvˌiˌlæstɪkˈkɔːd]	ein Stück Gummiseil
on the dotted line [ɒn ðə ˌdɒtɪd ˈlaɪn]	auf der gepunkteten Linie
to **sue** [suː]	verklagen
jump [dʒʌmp]	Sprung; Satz
to **be terrified (of sth)** [biː ˈterəfaɪd (əv)]	(große) Angst (vor etw.) haben
boulder [ˈbəʊldə]	Felsblock
check [tʃek]	Kontrolle
harness [ˈhɑːnɪs]	Gurtzeug; Geschirr
to **carry out** [ˌkæriˈaʊt]	ausführen; durchführen
doubt [daʊt]	Zweifel
to **chicken out** *(slang)* [ˌtʃɪkɪnˈaʊt]	kneifen
to **make contact** [ˌmeɪkˈkɒntækt]	berühren
to **yank** [jæŋk]	(ruckartig) ziehen; zerren
joy [dʒɔɪ]	Freude; Vergnügen
heart rate [ˈhɑːt ˌreɪt]	Herzfrequenz *(Puls)*
thrill-seeker [ˈθrɪlˌsiːkə]	*eine Person, die den Nervenkitzel sucht*

	zorbing [ˈzɔːbɪŋ]	Zorbing *(Funsport, bei dem man in einer aufblasbaren Kugel talabwärts rollt)*
p. 99	**skydiving** *(no pl)* [ˈskaɪˌdaɪvɪŋ]	Fallschirmspringen
	cliff [klɪf]	Klippe; Kliff
p. 100	**overrated** [ˌəʊvˈreɪtɪd]	überbewertet; überschätzt
	to **advise sb** [ədˈvaɪz]	jmdm. etw. raten; beraten
	backpacker [ˈbækpækə]	Rucksackreisender; Rucksackreisende

9 Put the words into the table.

chicken out · harness · boulder · overrated · yank · joy · inhabited · cliff · humorous · inactive · advise · sue

Nouns	Verbs	Adjectives

10 Complete the comments on the website.

My trip to Queenstown

My trip was a _____

(once-in-a-lifetime/joy) experience. When my girlfriend

suggested going _____ (boulder/

bungee-jumping), I wasn't sure if it was a good idea, but

now I'm so glad that I signed _____

(carried out/on the dotted line)! I can honestly say that

my _____ (heart rate/jump) has

never been so high!

Leanne, 21

I _____ (was terrified/had the time

of my life) in Queenstown and I can't wait to go back! My

friends and I went _____ (skydiving/

whitewater rafting) off a _____ (cliff/check) in

Queenstown. At the start I _____ (made

contact/was terrified) but I'm so happy that I

didn't _____ (chicken out/sue). We

also went _____ (the unknown/

zorbing), which was great fun.

Greg, 20

11 Find the words.

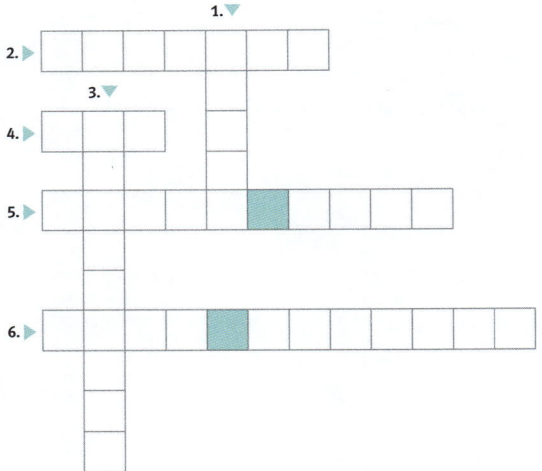

▼ 1. when you aren't sure
   3. something which isn't
      as good as people think

▶ 2. a large rock
   4. happiness or
      excitement
   5. how fast your heart
      is beating
   6. to touch something

12 Find the wrong word.

1. zorbing • backpacker • bungee jumping • canyoning

2. harness • length of elastic cord • ice cap • jump

3. boulder • jet lag • cliff • mountain

4. joy • chicken out • be terrified • run away

13 Complete the advert.

Are you a _____ ? Are you looking for a

once- _____ experience?

Then why not try _____ and experience

the pure _____ of flying and seeing the whole city

below you. If you have _____ about your safety,

there's no need to worry. We _____ all

the necessary _____ before

the _____. However, we _____ you

to read all the safety information on our website before you

register.

So what are you waiting for? Sign up and get ready to have

the _____ !

4

Text 2

p. 102	**rider** ['raɪdə]	Reiter; Reiterin
	best-selling [ˌbestˈselɪŋ]	Bestseller-; meistverkauft; meistgekauft
	chief [tʃiːf]	Häuptling
	heir [eə]	Erbe; Erbin
	bay [beɪ]	Bucht
	prayer [preə]	Gebet
	to **prove oneself** ['pruːv wʌnˌself]	sich selbst beweisen
	darkness *(no pl)* ['dɑːknəs]	Dunkelheit
	to **dive** [daɪv]	tauchen; springen
	to **lament** [ləˈment]	klagen
	veranda [vəˈrændə]	Veranda
	sandal ['sændl]	Sandale
	ribbon ['rɪbn]	Band
	pigtail ['pɪgteɪl]	Zopf
	to **nod** [nɒd]	nicken
	to **stand** [stænd]	*hier:* ertragen; ausstehen
p. 103	to **drop** [drɒp]	fallen (lassen)
	to **serve sb right** [ˌsɜːv ˈraɪt]	es verdient haben; jmdm. recht geschehen
	overboard ['əʊvəbɔːd]	über Bord
	breath [breθ]	Atem; Atemzug
	lung [lʌŋ]	Lunge
	to **yell** [jel]	brüllen; laut schreien
	to **take a deep breath** [ˌteɪk ə ˌdiːp ˈbreθ]	tief einatmen; tief Luft holen
	duck dive ['dʌk ˌdaɪv]	Duck-Dive *(Durchtauchmanöver)*
	stingray ['stɪŋreɪ]	Stachelrochen
	to **dog paddle** ['dɒg ˌpædl]	paddeln
	to **float** [fləʊt]	schweben; treiben
	sharp [ʃɑːp]	*hier:* plötzlich; scharf
	to **swallow** ['swɒləʊ]	schlucken
	surface ['sɜːfɪs]	Oberfläche

to **splutter** [ˈsplʌtə]	ausspucken; prusten; stottern
to **drown** [draʊn]	ertrinken
no matter [nəʊ ˈmætə]	egal; ganz gleich
to **kick** [kɪk]	schießen; treten
to **doubt** [daʊt]	bezweifeln
fat [fæt]	dick; fett
to **sink** [sɪŋk]	untergehen; sinken
to **search** [sɜːtʃ]	durchsuchen; suchen nach
panic [ˈpænɪk]	Panik
flash [flæʃ]	Blitz; Lichtblitz
p. 104 **satisfied** [ˈsætɪsfaɪd]	zufrieden; überzeugt
heart attack [ˈhɑːt ə̩tæk]	Herzinfarkt
crayfish [ˈkreɪfɪʃ]	Languste; Flusskrebs
silver [ˈsɪlvə]	Silber; silbern
to **tread water** [ˌtred ˈwɔːtə]	Wasser treten *(um aufrecht zu bleiben)*
to **blink** [blɪŋk]	blinzeln
carving [ˈkɑːvɪŋ]	Schnitzerei
portent [ˈpɔːtent]	Omen; Zeichen; Vorzeichen
to **tremble** [ˈtrembl]	zittern; beben
anticipation *(no pl)* [ænˌtɪsɪˈpeɪʃn]	Vorahnung; Erwartung
Let it be done. [ˌlet ɪt biː ˈdʌn]	Lass es geschehen.

14 Write the words in English.

1. _____

2. _____

3. _____

4. _____

15 Complete the sentences with the verbs in the right forms.

| lament | float | dive | nod | yell |

1. She put on her swimming costume and _____ into the sea.

2. When my sister is angry, she _____ at me.

3. While Paka _____, Kahu decided to go and get the stone.

4. When I asked him if he was alright, the old man just _____.

5. Does your boat _____?

16 Match the sentences parts.

1. They couldn't see anything in the
2. She dropped
3. The surface
4. He doubted that
5. The earrings were made of
6. The dog was trembling

a) pure silver.
b) they would arrive on time.
c) darkness.
d) because he was so scared.
e) of the lake was very calm.
f) a glass on the floor.

17 Complete the sentences and find the animal.

1. 'The Whale Rider' is a
   _ _ _ _ -☐_ _ _ _ _ _ novel.

2. It is about a girl who will not be _ _☐_ _ _ _ _ _
   until her family is happy.

3. Koro Apirana is the _ _☐_ _ of the tribe.

4 He is _ _ _ _ _ _ _☐ because none of the boys
   passed the test.

5. Kahu is wearing beautiful white ribbons in
   her _ _☐_ _ _ _ .

6. Kahu jumps _ _☐_ _ _ _ to get the stone for
   Koro Apirana.

7. Rawiri _☐_ _ _ _ for Kahu in the water.

8. Kahu not only finds the stone but also brings back a
   _ _ _☐_ _ _ for Koro Apirana.

☐☐☐☐☐☐☐☐

4

18 Find the words.

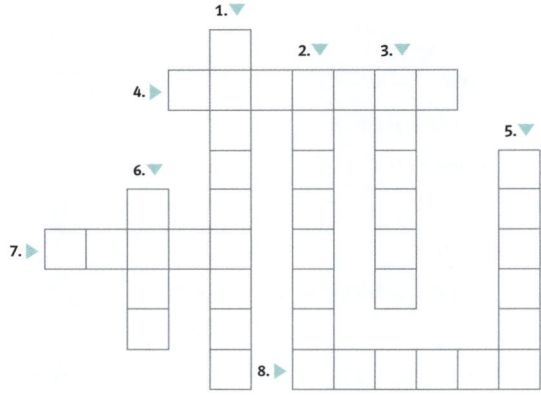

▼ 1. when you are pleased or happy with something
2. the opposite of light
3. to complain or be sad about something
5. the air that you take in through your mouth or nose
6. to move your foot very quickly

▶ 4. shoes that you wear in summer
7. the leader of a tribe
8. to look for something

When you are learning new words, think about how you would use them in a full sentence. This will help you to remember them better.

Zoom In – A world language

1 ▼ 1. native, 2. spoon, 3. audition
▶ 4. significant, 5. e-waste

2 1. cell phone, 2. sailor, 3. fork, 4. handbag

3 1. instance, 2. audition, 3. Even if, 4. store, 5. relatively, 6. auxiliary

Unit 1 – The rainbow nation

Intro

1 1. buffalo, 2. lion, 3. rhino, 4. leopard

2 World Cup, nation, unite, South Africans, apartheid, living conditions, exclusive, diverse

3 1. d, 2. e, 3. a, 4. c, 5. b

4 natural, lions, safari, nation, separated, unite

Topic 1

5 1. seal, 2. penguin, 3. running water, 4. dolphin

6 1. struck, 2. get by, 3. is rising, 4. made the most of, 5. reduce, 6. will be shown around

7 1. c, 2. d, 3. e, 4. f, 5. a, 6. b

8 1. backdrop, 2. coastline, 3. patrol, 4. plenty of, 5. cuisine, 6. perspective, 7. wealthy, 8. Unemployment, 9. carnival

9a residents, landline, income, flush, relaxed, access

9b relaxed, access, landline, flush, residents, income

10 1. minced meat, 2. survey, 3. unemployment, 4. resident

Topic 2

11 Nouns: inequality, neighbourhood, constitution, background
Verbs: cheer, marginalise, despise, last
Adjectives: calm, former, economic, remarkable

12 remarkable, lies ahead, shook hands, captain, democratic, cooperation, What's more, reaction, celebrations, fireworks

13 1. handshake/shake hands, 2. jersey, 3. fireworks, 4. politician

14 democratic, economic, politicians, cooperation, Personally, constitution, inequality, marginalised

15 1. marginalise, 2. went wild, 3. lie ahead, 4. shook hands,
5. fills up

16 1. e, 2. a, 3. f, 4. b, 5. d, 6. c

Text 2

17 Nouns: determination, wife, duty
Verbs: heal, pronounce, retire
Adjectives: fair, unexpected, extraordinary

18 announced, extraordinary, regard, overcame, determination,
released, justice, campaigned, well-known

19 welcome, impact, divorced, funeral, extraordinary, released,
publicity, retire, public, named, raised, remind, campaign

Unit 2 – Living in a global village

Intro

1 1. Mandarin, 2. Arabic, 3. planet, 4. senior

2 planet, refugees, due to, floods, droughts, overweight, obese,
literacy, illiterate

3 Nouns: half, planet, a third
Verbs: identify, disappear, remain
Adjectives: illiterate, overweight, healthy

4 1. f, 2. g, 3. e, 4. c, 5. d, 6. a, 7. b

Topic 1

5 vertical garden, given the green light, environmentally friendly,
environmental, Unless, harmful, justify, costs, As far as I can
see, sustainable, ensure, wasted, biodiversity, absorb, in favour
of, turns out

6 1. d, 2. h, 3. b, 4. g, 5. e, 6. a, 7. c, 8. f

7 1. pea, 2. square, 3. package, 4. motorway

8 1. biodiversity, 2. harmful, 3. vertical garden, 4. encourage

9 schemes, sustainable, architects, ensure, environmentally
friendly, waste, landfill sites, packaging, encourage,
environmental

Topic 2

10 1. medication, 2. contract, 3. meet, 4. Asian, 5. trade

11 1. meet, 2. signed, 3. punished, 4. differ, 5. take action,
6. worries

12 1. e, 2. c, 3. d, 4. a, 5. b

13 source, damage, backward, inappropriate, fake news, necessary

14 1. f, 2. g, 3. a, 4. c, 5. b, 6. e, 7. d

15 trade, medical, production, pandemic, If the worst comes to the
worst, medication, sources, definitely, healthcare, in case, By
the way, take action, sign, petition

Text 2

16 effect, conference, talks, themes, mobility, security, concepts,
give us a call, venue, in person

17 1. fit, 2. mobility, 3. placard, 4. effect, 5. participant,
6. smuggle, 7. venue, 8. theme, 9. Brazil, → foreigner

18 1. sole, 2. technical, 3. Brazil, 4. cheek

19 1. d, 2. f, 3. e, 4. g, 5. b, 6. a, 7. c

20 It's a shame, conference, annoying, After all, theme, mobility,
talk, effects, have a point, in person, apart, technical,
all in all

Look at Literature – Visions of another world

1 1. handsome, 2. fantasy, 3. vision, 4. reality, 5. moral,
6. utopian, 7. professional, 8. tale, → dystopia

2 1. break free, 2. is in charge of, 3. handled, 4. reflects,
5. criticised, 6. are set in, 7. questions, 8. got into trouble

3 marks, flawed, criticise, occurs, ethical, question

4 dystopian, idea, constant, observed, space, moral, criticise

5 1. e, 2. g, 3. a, 4. b, 5. f, 6. c, 7. d

Unit 3 – International work and trade

Intro

1 translator, number of, freelance, banking, cost of living, move in with, was made redundant, devastated, course, accounting, interests

2 ▼ 1. Syria, 3. for good, 5. parcel
   ▶ 2. outsource, 4. grateful, 6. boomtown, 7. devastated

Topic 1

3 Nouns: density, arrival, port
   Verbs: relax, browse, swap
   Adjectives: major, populated, dense

4 image, taxes, imported, position, gateway, governmental, handed back

5 Cantonese, dialect, dense, Consequently, upwards, major, range, relax, browse

6 1. over, 2. into, 3. over, 4. out, 5. off

7 1. headphones, 2. luggage, 3. toy

8 a) hectic, legal, import, luggage, chilly, harmony, toy

8 b) 1. toy, 2. chilly, 3. harmony, 4. legal, 5. luggage, 6. import,
       7. hectic

Topic 2

9 complaint, order, refund, within, Yours faithfully, apology, order, supervisor, complaint, look into, get back to me, within

10 1. thread, 2. cupboard, 3. cushion, 4. coat, 5. jumper,
    6. mattress, 7. shorts, 8. tights

11 1. thread, 2. chemical, 3. urgent, 4. fabric

12 1. supervisor, 2. confirmation, 3. cotton, 4. donation, 5. fabric

13 1. thrilled, 2. renewable, 3. organic, 4. vegan, 5. unsafe,
    6. toxic, 7. trained, 8. urgent

14 1. d, 2. f, 3. c, 4. e, 5. b, 6. a

15 rethink, urgent, greenhouse gas emissions, refashion, donates, jumper, cushion, compress, filling, mattresses, donation, instead of

16 rent, instead of, donate, trained, organic, launched, chemicals, microplastics, unsafe, working conditions, matches

Text 2

17 1. c, 2. f, 3. d, 4. e, 5. a, 6. b

18 1. alarm, 2. pirate, 3. chest, 4. speedboat

19 bound for, pirates, officer, spotted, radioed, on board, shipping containers, cargo, route, risk, keep track of, progress (position)

20 ▼ 1. register, 2. rare, 4. risk, 5. pitch, 6. exist
   ▶ 3. board, 7. pirate, 8. Sunset

21 cabin, boarded, deck, sunset, spotted, on board, Malaysian, curry, admit

Unit 4 – Kia ora, New Zealand!

Intro

1 enthusiasts, fjords, subtropical, rugged, filmmakers, adrenaline junkies, abseiling, volunteers

2 1. filmmaker, 2. abseiling, 3. tail, 4. flow

3 1. enthusiast, 2. literally, 3. Maori, 4. topic, 5. approximately, 6. TV station, 7. headed, 8. earthquakes, 9. stopover

Topic 1

4 1. d, 2. f, 3. c, 4. b, 5. g, 6. e, 7. a

5 brochure, breathtaking, yet, peace and quiet, rainforests, unsurprisingly, consider, scenic, telescope, binoculars, glow-worms, light up, Plus, Above all, footprints

6 1. kiwi, 2. gnome, 3. footprint, 4. telescope

7 1. stick to, 2. convinced, 3. considering, 4. cracks jokes, 5. generated, 6. assumes

8 Honestly, in the first place, trilogy, sense of humour, scenic, disciplined, traffic light, assumed, chaotic

Topic 2

9 Nouns: harness, boulder, joy, cliff
Verbs: chicken out, yank, advise, sue
Adjectives: overrated, inhabited, humorous, inactive

10 once-in-a-lifetime, bungee-jumping, on the dotted line, heart rate, had the time of my life, skydiving, cliff, was terrified, chicken out, zorbing

11 ▼ 1. doubt, 3. overrated
  ▶ 2. boulder, 4. joy, 5. heart rate, 6. make contact

12 1. backpacker, 2. ice cap, 3. jet lag, 4. joy

13 thrill-seeker, in-a-lifetime, skydiving, joy, doubts, carry out, checks, jump, advise, the time of your life

Text 2

14 1. sandal, 2. ribbon, 3. stingray, 4. bay

15 1. dived, 2. yells, 3. was lamenting, 4. nodded, 5. float

16 1. c, 2. f, 3. e, 4. b, 5. a, 6. d

17 1. best-selling, 2. satisfied, 3. chief, 4. lamenting, 5. pigtails, 6. overboard, 7. searches, 8. crayfish → stingray

18 ▼ 1. satisfied, 2. darkness, 3. lament, 5. breath, 6. kick
  ▶ 4. sandals, 7. chief, 8. search